ILLUSTRATED LIBRARY OF COOKING

VOLUME **6** Coo-Cou

FIVE *books in one: a handy collection of menus and recipes for just two people ...another collection for coping with crowds...a third for cooking on boats or in backwoods...still another for the charcoal chef...and finally, a comprehensive diet guide that includes everything every dieter needs to know on becoming his old self again.*

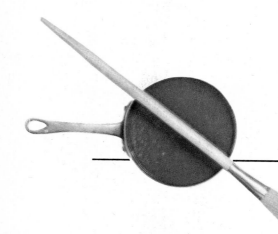

ROCKVILLE HOUSE PUBLISHERS, INC.
ROCKVILLE CENTRE, NEW YORK 11570

VOLUME **6**

Family Circle®

Illustrated Library of

COOKING

YOUR READY REFERENCE FOR A LIFETIME OF GOOD EATING

Picture Credits:

Best Foods, a Division of CPC International • National Live Stock & Meat Board • George Nordhausen • Pacific Kitchen • Reynolds Wrap

Ever an alfresco favorite: crispy coleslaw, shown here with tart apple crescents.

Table of Contents

COOKING FOR A CROWD

COOKING FOR A CROWD: BEEF BUFFET, HAM BUFFET, SMORGASBORD AN ALFRESCO FEAST, A COLLECTION OF CROWD PLEASERS

"You entertain so easily!" How often have you heard this compliment, repeated it yourself, or had the bouquet pinned on you? For it is *you*, the hostess, who sets the mood of your party. Being relaxed and gracious when entertaining is an easy reputation to build with everything well in hand—and, with a plan, it *can* be. Here's the secret: Before you invite anyone, sit down where it's quiet and just dream through your party, making notes as you go. Use these planning tips as your guide, then turn the pages for all kinds of food ideas.

Whether it's a supper buffet or outdoor party for someone special, limit the guest list to the number you can accommodate comfortably.

Choose guests with common interests or who "go together" well. If one is a shy type, plan to have her meet an outgoing counterpart. If someone is new to the group, drop a hint of her interests in your introduction as a starting point for conversation.

647

A bang-up buffet for 25 people. Herbed Beef Roast stars along with two-toned Seafood Salad Soufflé in a showy mold.

COOKING FOR A CROWD

Telephone or write a note, as you wish, but make it at least a week in advance, longer around the holidays when more parties are being given. Be specific on date, time, place, what to wear (if it's a theme party), and your plan for any special activity—a swim, cookout, or bridge.

Organize Your Party Plans

First, start with the menu. If you are to do all the cooking, keep it simple and easy to serve. A meal as plain as a casserole main dish, crisp green salad, ice-cream dessert, and coffee can be made ahead, and needs little last-minute attention. Yet, with a few bright garnishes, it can be quite partylike. It's best not to attempt a dish you have never tried before. Instead, give it a preview for the family. They'll like the surprise and you'll have the practice.

Make up a shopping list. Buy staples ahead, perishables the day before to take advantage of what is freshest in the supermarket.

Post the menu with a cooking schedule. Include what can be done a day or even two ahead, how much time to allow to cook or heat the food, what will need to be done, just before serving time. Then check off each step as you do it.

Check linen, silver, and china. Decide which serving dish to use for each food. If your party is too large for your supply, ask to borrow extras from a friend. On the day of your party, lay out everything, including accessories such as salt and pepper shakers, so they can be moved quickly to your serving spot.

Plan a centerpiece. A fancy flower and candle decoration looks lovely, but a simple bowl of fruit (to double with cheese for dessert) or a bouquet of flowers from your own garden is quite enough.

Save time for yourself. Allow at least an hour before the party to dress leisurely, so you'll be ready to greet your guests, relaxed and eager to enjoy the fun.

BEEF BUFFET FOR 25

Herbed Beef Roast with Chutney
Fruit Sauce and Mustard Cream
Parker House Midgets
Molded Cheese Pineapple
Seafood Salad Soufflé
Appetizer Vegetables
Tiny Tim Pecan Tarts with fresh and candied fruits and nuts
Strawberry Fruit-Cup Punch

Herbed Beef Roast

Carve this favorite into small thin slices to top with a zippy spread and pop into a tiny oven-warm bun.
Roast at 325° for 2¼ hours. Makes 25 servings

1 beef eye-round roast, weighing from 5 to 6 pounds
½ cup sifted all-purpose flour
3 teaspoons salt
1 teaspoon paprika

Zooming in for a close-up of savory Herbed Beef Roast.

1 teaspoon leaf basil, crumbled
1 teaspoon leaf marjoram, crumbled
Watercress

1 Place roast on a sheet of wax paper. Mix remaining ingredients, except watercress, in a cup; pat well into roast. Place on a rack in a shallow baking pan. If using a meat thermometer, insert bulb into thickest part of roast. Do not add water or cover pan.
2 Roast in slow oven (325°) 2¼ hours, or until thermometer registers 140° for rare. Cover pan loosely with foil; let stand at room temperature until serving time.
3 Carve about one third of the roast into very thin slices; cut each slice in three or four pieces. Arrange pieces, along with remaining roast, on a serving platter. Garnish platter with watercress and top roast with a bouquet of radish roses, if you wish. Serve with MUSTARD CREAM and CHUTNEY FRUIT SAUCE *(both recipes follow)*.
Hostess Note—Roast tastes equally inviting served cold, so cook it the day before or morning of your party, if you wish.

Chutney Fruit Sauce
Canned peaches blend with onion and zippy spices for this savory meat spread.
Makes 2 cups

1 can (1 pound, 13 ounces) cling-peach slices
1 small onion, chopped (¼ cup)
¼ teaspoon ground cumin
⅛ teaspoon ground allspice
½ teaspoon Worcestershire sauce
¼ teaspoon liquid red pepper seasoning
2 tablespoons lemon juice

1 Drain syrup from peaches into a cup. Measure 2 tablespoonfuls and combine with peaches, onion, cumin, allspice, Worcestershire sauce, and red pepper seasoning in an electric-blender container; cover. Beat at high speed 1 minute, or until smooth; pour into a small saucepan.
2 Heat to boiling, then simmer, stirring often, 5 minutes to blend flavors; remove from heat.
3 Stir in lemon juice; chill.
Hostess Note—If you do not have a blender, place peaches in a small deep bowl and beat with an electric beater until smooth. Mince onion, then combine with peaches and remaining ingredients. Sauce may not be quite so smooth, but it will taste just as good. Another tip: Although sauce may be made ahead, it tastes best slightly warm, so remove it from refrigerator and let stand at room temperature for an hour before serving.

Mustard Cream
Flavor is delicate and just spicy enough for succulent roast beef.
Makes about 2 cups

1 cup mayonnaise or salad dressing
½ cup prepared mustard
½ cup canned condensed beef consommé
¼ cup light cream or table cream

Combine all ingredients in a medium-size bowl; beat with an electric or rotary beater until well blended. Chill.
Hostess Note—Sauce keeps well, so make it a day ahead and store, covered, in the refrigerator.

Molded Cheese Pineapple
Such a conversation piece! And it's so worth the splurge on a fresh pineapple to get the stately crown.
Makes 25 servings

1½ pounds sharp Cheddar cheese, grated (6 cups)
½ pound Swiss cheese, grated (2 cups)
1 package (8 ounces) cream cheese, softened
¼ pound blue cheese, crumbled
½ cup (1 stick) butter or margarine, softened
½ cup apple juice
2 tablespoons lemon juice
1 tablespoon Worcestershire sauce
Whole cloves
Paprika
1 leafy crown from a large fresh pineapple

1 Combine Cheddar, Swiss, cream, and blue cheeses with butter or margarine in the large bowl of an electric mixer. Slowly beat in apple and lemon juices, and Worcestershire sauce; continue beating, scraping down side of bowl often, 5 minutes, or until well blended; cover. Chill several hours, or until firm enough to handle.
2 Shape cheese mixture with your hands into a "pineapple" on a plate; smooth top flat; cover with foil, transparent wrap, or wax paper. Chill several hours, or until very firm.
3 Before serving, mark cheese all over with the tip of a teaspoon to resemble a pineapple; center each mark with a whole clove; lightly sprinkle cheese with paprika. Lift mold onto a serving plate with a pancake turner.
4 Place pineapple crown on top of mold; hold in place with several wooden picks, if needed. Frame with party-size pumpernickel and your favorite crisp crackers, if you wish.
Hostess Note—If there's any cheese left, remove

649

pineapple crown and discard. Cover cheese well and keep chilled. It will stay fresh-tasting for a week or more.

Seafood Salad Soufflé
No need to serve extra dressing with this beauty, for it's molded into both layers.
Makes 25 servings

Lime Layer
1 package (3 ounces) lime-flavor gelatin
1 cup hot water
1 cup (8-ounce carton) dairy sour cream
½ cup mayonnaise or salad dressing
2 tablespoons lemon juice
½ teaspoon salt
   Few drops liquid red pepper seasoning
1 large cucumber

Seafood Layer
2 envelopes unflavored gelatin
1½ cups water
2 cans (1 pound each) salmon
1 can (about 7 ounces) crabmeat
½ cup mayonnaise or salad dressing
2 tablespoons lemon juice
1 teaspoon salt
¼ teaspoon freshly ground pepper
2 egg whites
1 cup cream for whipping
   Red food coloring

1 Make lime layer: Dissolve lime-flavor gelatin in hot water in a medium-size bowl; stir in sour cream, mayonnaise or salad dressing, lemon juice, salt, and red pepper seasoning. Chill 30 minutes, or until as thick as unbeaten egg white.
2 Cut about 12 thin even slices from cucumber, then trim a sliver from each so it will stand flat around edge of mold; set aside for Step 8. Pare remaining cucumber and trimmings and chop fine; fold into thickened lime-gelatin mixture; pour into a 12-cup fancy tube mold. Chill 30 minutes, or just until sticky-firm.
3 While mixture in mold chills, make seafood layer: Soften gelatin in ½ cup of the water in a small saucepan; heat, stirring constantly, until gelatin dissolves; remove from heat. Stir in remaining 1 cup water.
4 Drain both cans of salmon; bone and flake into a medium-size bowl. Drain crab meat; flake and remove bony tissue, if any; add to salmon.

5 Combine ⅓ each of the seafood and gelatin mixtures at a time in an electric-blender container; cover. Beat at high speed until smooth; pour into a large bowl. Stir in mayonnaise or salad dressing, lemon juice, salt, and pepper.
6 Beat egg whites until they stand in firm peaks in a small bowl. Beat cream until stiff in a medium-size bowl. Fold beaten egg whites, then whipped cream into seafood mixture. Tint salmon color with a few drops food coloring. Carefully spoon over sticky-firm layer in mold. Chill several hours, or until firm. (Overnight is best.)
7 When ready to serve, run a sharp-tip, thin-blade knife around top of salad, then dip mold *very quickly* in and out of a pan of hot water. Cover mold with a serving plate; turn upside down; gently lift off mold.
8 Stand saved cucumber slices, flat edge down, around side of salad. Fill center with a few crisp romaine or curly endive leaves, if you wish.

Parker House Midgets
Each of these buttery gems is just the right size to make into a two-bite sandwich.
Bake at 450° for 15 minutes. Makes 80 tiny rolls

½ cup (1 stick) butter or margarine
4 packages refrigerated plain or buttermilk biscuits

1 Melt butter or margarine in a jelly-roll pan, 15x10x1, while oven heats.
2 Separate the 10 biscuits in each package; cut each in half. (Scissors make the job go fast.) Roll each half into a tiny ball, then flatten with a glass to a 2-inch round; fold round in half.
3 Roll in melted butter or margarine in pan to coat all over, then arrange in a single layer in same pan. (So rolls keep a trim neat shape, arrange in 10 rows of eight each.)
4 Bake in very hot oven (450°) 15 minutes, or until golden. Serve hot.
Hostess Note—Rolls may be baked ahead, if you wish, then reheated just before serving time.

Appetizer Vegetables
Tart lemon butter turns crisply cooked vegetables into a delightfully different titbit.
Makes 25 servings

1 bunch broccoli (about 2 pounds)
1 medium-size cauliflower
2 packages (9 ounces each) frozen artichoke hearts
2 tablespoons finely chopped onion
½ cup (1 stick) butter or margarine
¼ teaspoon salt
¼ teaspoon paprika
3 tablespoons lemon juice
   Diced pimiento

1 Cut broccoli flowerets from stems, saving stems to cook for another meal; halve large flowerets. Trim green leafy stems from cauliflower; break cauliflower into flowerets; halve any large ones.
2 Cook both vegetables, covered, in boiling salted water in separate large saucepans 8 minutes, or just until crisply tender; drain. Cook artichoke hearts, following label directions; drain. Keep all hot.
3 Sauté onion in butter or margarine in a small frying pan 2 minutes; remove from heat. Stir in salt, paprika, and lemon juice.
4 When ready to serve, arrange artichoke hearts at either end of a large chafing dish or keep-hot server; arrange broccoli and cauliflowerets in center. Drizzle lemon butter over all. Sprinkle artichoke hearts with pimiento.

Tiny Tim Pecan Tarts
Filling is similar to pecan pie—and just sweet enough for a light party top-off.
Bake at 375° for 20 minutes. Makes 3 dozen

1 package piecrust mix
3 eggs
¾ cup sugar
¼ teaspoon salt
1 cup dark corn syrup
1 teaspoon vanilla
3 tablespoons all-purpose flour
1 cup cream for whipping
   Pecan halves

1 Prepare piecrust mix, following label directions, or make pastry from your favorite dou-

ble-crust recipe. Roll out, half at a time, to a rectangle, 14x10, on a lightly floured pastry cloth or board. Cut out 12 rounds with a 3-inch plain or scalloped cutter.
2 Fit each round into a tiny muffin-pan cup, pressing firmly against bottom and side. Repeat with remaining half of dough; reroll trimmings and cut out to make 36 shells in all.
3 Beat eggs slightly in a medium-size bowl; stir in sugar, salt, corn syrup, and vanilla, then flour. Spoon about 1 tablespoonful into each shell.
4 Bake in moderate oven (375°) 20 minutes, or until pastry is golden and filling is set. Cool in pans on wire racks 10 minutes, then remove carefully; cool completely.
5 Just before serving, beat cream until stiff in a small bowl. Spoon a dollop on top of each tart; decorate each with a pecan half.
Hostess Note—Tarts may be baked the day before your party, if you wish. Place in a single layer in a jelly-roll pan or on a cookie sheet and cover with transparent wrap or wax paper. Store in a cool dry place.

Strawberry Fruit-Cup Punch
It looks so inviting on your party table. Flavor is slightly sweet yet tangy.
Makes 25 servings, about 1 cup each

9 packages (10 ounces each) frozen sliced strawberries, partly thawed
¾ cup currant jelly
¾ cup lime juice
6 cups finely crushed ice
6 cups water
1 large lime, sliced thin

1 Combine 3 packages of the strawberries, ¼ cup of the currant jelly, and ¼ cup of the lime juice in an electric-blender container; cover. Beat until smooth; pour into a large punch bowl. Repeat two more times with remaining berries, jelly, and lime juice.
2 Stir in ice and water until well blended. Float lime slices on top. Serve in punch cups or dainty glasses.
Hostess Note—If your punch bowl is small, mix punch, one third at a time, and refill bowl as needed.

HAM BUFFET FOR 25

Buffet Glazed Ham
Sweet-Sour Mustard Cream
Button Biscuits
Meat Ball Miniatures
Dilled Relish Tray
Pâté-Cheese Mold
Crisp Crackers
Candlelight Cake
Holiday Punch

Holiday Punch
Its cool green color adds a festive note to your party table.
Makes 50 punch-cup servings

1 cup sugar
1 two-inch piece of stick cinnamon
5 whole cloves
5 whole allspice
2 cups water
2 cans (6 ounces each) frozen concentrate for lemonade
2 cans (6 ounces each) frozen concentrate for limeade
2 bottles (1 pint, 12 ounces each) quinine water, chilled
2 bottles (1 pint, 12 ounces each) carbonated water, chilled
ICE BLOCK (directions follow)

1 Combine sugar, cinnamon stick, cloves, allspice, and water in a small saucepan; heat to boiling; simmer 5 minutes. Strain into a medium-size bowl; cool.
2 When ready to mix punch, pour spiced-water mixture into a punch bowl; stir in frozen lemonade and limeade, and quinine and carbonated waters.
3 Float ice block on top. Surround bowl with clusters of green grapes, as pictured, if you wish.
ICE BLOCK—The day before the party, fill a fancy mold that will fit into the punch bowl with water; freeze. To unmold, dip quickly in and out of a pan of hot water; float on top of punch. Garnish with a ring of alternating slices of lemon and lime.

653

Great way to serve a crowd of friends: sliced-before-cooking Buffet Glazed Ham with Meat Ball Miniatures and Pâté-Cheese Mold to round out the festive menu.

Meat Ball Miniatures

Flavorful beef and mild veal go into these titbits to serve in a gingery sauce.
Makes 25 servings

2 pounds ground beef
2 pounds ground veal
½ cup sifted all-purpose flour
½ teaspoon ground ginger
1 cup light cream or table cream
¼ cup soy sauce
4 tablespoons (½ stick) butter or margarine
  GINGER SOY SAUCE (recipe follows)
2 medium-size green peppers
1 can (5 ounces) water chestnuts

1 Combine ground beef and veal, flour, and ginger in the large bowl of an electric mixer; beat until blended, then beat in cream and soy sauce, 1 tablespoon at a time, until mixture is smooth and pastelike.
2 Shape into tiny balls. (This amount will make as many as 180 marble-size balls. Shaping can be done ahead and balls chilled until ready to cook.)
3 Sauté meat balls, a single layer at a time, in part of the butter or margarine until cooked through in a large frying pan. Keep hot while cooking remaining meat balls, adding remaining butter or margarine as needed, and making GINGER SOY SAUCE.
4 Quarter green peppers; remove seeds; cut peppers in small squares. Drain water chestnuts; cut in thin slices.
5 Pour GINGER SOY SAUCE into a chafing dish or keep-hot server. Spoon meat balls on top, basting with sauce; tuck in green peppers and water chestnuts. Serve with wooden picks for spearing meat balls.
  GINGER SOY SAUCE—After all meat balls are cooked, tip pan so fat will rise to top; pour off all fat, leaving brown drippings in pan. Measure ¼ cup fat and return to pan; blend in ¼ cup flour and ¼ teaspoon ground ginger; cook, stirring constantly, just until bubbly. Stir in 2 cups water and 3 tablespoons soy sauce; continue cooking and stirring, scraping cooked-on bits from bottom and side of pan, until sauce thickens and boils 1 minute. Makes about 2 cups.

Dilled Relish Tray

Such a good keeper that it can be made days ahead.
Makes 25 servings

2 large Bermuda onions
4 medium-size cucumbers
2 cans (3 or 4 ounces each) mushroom caps
1¾ cups sugar
4 teaspoons salt
2 teaspoons dillweed
2 cups white vinegar
1 cup water

1 Peel onions; slice thin and separate into rings; place in a large bowl. Pare cucumbers and score with a fork; slice cucumbers thin; place in a medium-size bowl. Drain liquid from mushrooms and save for soup or gravy; place mushrooms in a small bowl.
2 Combine sugar, salt, dillweed, vinegar, and water in a medium-size saucepan; heat to boiling. Pour over vegetables in each bowl; cover. Chill several hours or overnight.
3 When ready to serve, remove vegetables from liquid with a slotted spoon. Pile into a sectioned relish tray or into separate small bowls.

Buffet Glazed Ham

This no-carve baked ham boasts a handsome fruit glaze and a Della Robbia crown.
Bake at 325° for 2 hours and 30 minutes

For 25 generous servings, plus some for a bonus dish or two, buy an about-10-pound canned boneless ready-to-eat ham. Ask your meatman to slice it into ¼-inch-thick slices, keeping it in its original shape, then tie securely with string. (During slow shopping hours he will be glad to do this.) When ready to heat, place ham in a large shallow baking pan. Bake in slow oven (325°) 2 hours; spread part of the CURRANT GLAZE (recipe follows) over top. Continue baking, basting with more glaze, 30 minutes longer, or until ham is richly glazed. Place on a heated serving platter or tray; cut away strings. Garnish top of ham with a crown of marzipan fruits and halved pecans, and frame with watercress, as pictured.
  CURRANT GLAZE—Combine 1 cup currant jelly with 2 tablespoons lemon juice and ½ teaspoon pumpkin-pie spice in a small saucepan. Heat, stirring constantly, just until well-blended. Makes about 1 cup.

Sweet-Sour Mustard Cream
Spread this zippy-seasoned sauce on the ham, and pop into a tiny biscuit.
Makes about 1 cup

    2 tablespoons butter or margarine
    2 tablespoons all-purpose flour
    2 tablespoons dry mustard
    1 tablespoon sugar
    1 teaspoon salt
      Dash of cayenne
    1 cup milk
    1 egg, beaten
    2 tablespoons cider vinegar

1 Melt butter or margarine in a medium-size saucepan; stir in flour, mustard, sugar, salt, and cayenne. Cook, stirring constantly, just until bubbly. Stir in milk; continue cooking and stirring until sauce thickens and boils 1 minute.
2 Stir ½ cup of the hot mixture into beaten egg in a small bowl, then stir back into remaining sauce in pan; cook, stirring constantly, 1 minute longer. Remove from heat; stir in vinegar.
3 Cool, then chill. Just before serving, beat until smooth.

Button Biscuits
Bake these dainty biscuits, part at a time, to keep them coming piping hot.
Bake at 450° for 12 minutes. Makes 4 dozen

    4 cups sifted all-purpose flour
    6 tablespoons baking powder
    2 teaspoons sugar
    1 teaspoon salt
    ½ cup vegetable shortening
    1½ cups milk

1 Sift flour, baking powder, sugar, and salt into a large bowl; cut in shortening with a pastry blender until mixture is crumbly; stir in milk to make a soft dough.
2 Turn out onto a lightly floured pastry cloth or board; knead gently ½ minute. Roll out to a rectangle ½ inch thick; cut into rounds with a 1½-inch cutter; place on greased cookie sheets. Reroll and cut out all trimmings.

3 Bake in very hot oven (450°) 12 minutes, or until golden.

Pâté-Cheese Mold
A stuffed-olive crown sparkles atop this holiday meat-cheese pleaser.
Makes 25 servings

Meat Layer
    1 envelope unflavored gelatin
    1 envelope instant chicken broth
      OR: 1 chicken-bouillon cube
    1 cup water
    1 tablespoon lemon juice
    3 large stuffed green olives, sliced
    ½ pound bologna
    ¼ cup mayonnaise or salad dressing
    ¼ cup sweet-mustard relish (from a 9-ounce jar)

Cheese Layer
    1 envelope unflavored gelatin
    ¼ cup water
    2 wedges (1⅓ ounces each) Camembert
      cheese
    ¼ pound blue cheese
    ¼ teaspoon curry powder
    1 egg, separated
    1 cup (8-ounce carton) dairy sour cream
      Green food coloring

1 Make meat layer: Soften gelatin with chicken broth or bouillon cube in water in a small saucepan. Heat, stirring constantly and crushing cube, if using, with a spoon, just until gelatin dissolves. Measure ¼ cup into a 6-cup mold; stir in lemon juice. (Keep remaining gelatin mixture at room temperature.)
2 Set mold in a pan of ice and water to speed setting; chill just until syrupy-thick. Arrange stuffed-olive slices in gelatin to make a pretty pattern. Chill until sticky-firm.
3 While mold chills, remove skin from bologna; put meat through a food chopper, using a fine blade. Mix with remaining gelatin mixture, mayonnaise or salad dressing, and relish in a medium-size bowl; spoon over sticky-firm olive layer in mold. Continue chilling in same pan of ice and water until sticky-firm while making cheese layer.
4 Make cheese layer: Soften gelatin in water in a small saucepan; heat slowly just until gelatin dissolves.
5 Beat Camembert and blue cheeses until

655

well blended in a medium-size bowl; beat in curry powder, egg yolk, and dissolved gelatin.

6 Beat egg white until it stands in firm peaks in a small bowl. Fold into cheese mixture, then fold in sour cream. Tint mixture light green with a drop or two of food coloring.

7 Spoon over sticky-firm meat layer in mold; cover with wax paper, foil, or transparent wrap. Chill in refrigerator several hours, or until firm. (Overnight is best.)

8 When ready to unmold, run a sharp-tip, thin-blade knife around top of mold, then dip mold *very quickly* in and out of a pan of hot water. Cover mold with a serving plate; turn upside down; gently lift off mold. Surround with your choice of crisp crackers.

Candlelight Cake

Fluffy whipped cream baked right in the cake adds extra moistness. For a festive touch, stand a lighted candle in the center hole.
Bake at 325° for 1 hour and 15 minutes. Makes one 10-inch tube cake

    2¾ cups sifted cake flour
     4 teaspoons baking powder
     1 teaspoon salt
     4 eggs, separated
    1¾ cups sugar
     1 cup cream for whipping
     1 teaspoon vanilla
     1 teaspoon almond extract
     ⅔ cup milk
       10X (confectioners' powdered) sugar

1 Measure cake flour, baking powder, and salt into a sifter.

2 Beat egg whites until foamy-light and double in volume in a medium-size bowl; beat in ½ cup of the sugar, 1 tablespoon at a time, beating all the time until meringue forms soft peaks. (Set remaining 1¼ cups sugar aside for Step 4.)

3 Beat cream until stiff in a medium-size bowl; chill.

4 Beat egg yolks until creamy-thick in a large bowl; beat in remaining 1¼ cups sugar, 1 tablespoon at a time, beating all the time until mixture is fluffy-light. Beat in vanilla and almond extract.

5 Sift in flour mixture, adding alternately with milk and stirring just until well-blended; fold in meringue and whipped cream until no streaks of white remain. Pour into a greased and floured

10-cup fancy tube mold or a 10-inch angel-cake pan.

6 Bake in slow oven (325°) 1 hour and 15 minutes, or until top springs back when lightly pressed with fingertip.

7 Cool in pan on a wire rack 15 minutes; loosen around edge and tube with a knife, then invert onto a serving plate.

8 When ready to serve, dust lightly with 10X sugar and top with a ring of sliced pistachio nuts, if you wish. Cut into 1-inch-thick wedges.

SMORGASBORD FOR 12

Glazed Liver Pâté
Scandinavian Appetizer Tray
Salmon Mousse in Aspic
Fish Balls with Parsley Sauce
Turkey-Ham Galantine
Sweet-Sour Brown Beans
Dilled Potato-Salad Platter
Caraway Cabbage Toss
Assorted Breads and Crackers
Dessert Cheese Tray
Lingonberry Torte
Swedish Apple Cake

Glazed Liver Pâté

Bake at 350° for 2 hours. Makes 12 servings

    2 pounds calf's liver
    ½ pound sliced bacon, cut in 1-inch pieces
    1 medium-size onion, chopped (½ cup)
    1 clove of garlic, sliced
    1 envelope instant chicken broth
    1 bay leaf
    ½ teaspoon ground allspice
    ½ teaspoon leaf thyme, crumbled
    1 cup cream for whipping
    1 can (2 ounces) anchovy fillets
    ¼ cup sifted all-purpose flour
    ¼ teaspoon salt
    ¼ teaspoon pepper
    2 eggs
    2 tablespoons brandy
    1 envelope unflavored gelatin
    1 can (10½ ounces) condensed beef broth
      Carrot, green onion, and pitted ripe olives

For a dozen close friends: Scandinavian Smorgasbord.

1 Two days before your party, bake liver loaf. Grease a loaf pan, 9x5x3; line with double-thick foil, leaving a 3-inch overhang all around.
2 Wash liver; cut into 2-inch pieces. Combine with bacon, onion, garlic, chicken broth, bay leaf, allspice, and thyme in a large frying pan; cover. (Do not add water.) Simmer, stirring several times, 30 minutes; remove bay leaf.
3 Pour half of mixture into an electric-blender container; add half of the cream and anchovies with oil; beat until smooth. Pour into a large bowl. Repeat with remaining liver mixture, cream, and anchovies.
4 Stir in flour, salt, and pepper; beat in eggs and brandy. Spoon into prepared pan; fold ends of foil over top.
5 Set pan in a larger pan on oven shelf; pour boiling water into pan to a depth of about 1 inch.
6 Bake in moderate oven (350°) 2 hours. Remove from water; chill overnight.
7 One day before your party, glaze loaf. Sprinkle gelatin over half of the beef broth in a small saucepan; heat, stirring constantly, until gelatin dissolves; remove from heat. Stir in remaining broth; cool.
8 Loosen chilled loaf around edges of pan with a knife; peel back foil and lift loaf from pan; peel off foil.
9 Cut flower, leaf, and stem shapes from carrot, onion, and olives. Wash pan and dry; place in a larger pan of ice and water to speed setting.
10 Pour ½ cup of the gelatin mixture into pan; chill just until sticky-firm. Arrange cutouts in a pretty pattern on sticky-firm gelatin. Carefully spoon in just enough more gelatin mixture to cover vegetables; let set until sticky-firm.
11 Place liver loaf carefully over gelatin in pan; pour in all remaining gelatin mixture. Remove from ice. Chill in refrigerator overnight.
12 When ready to serve, run a sharp-tip thin-blade knife around top of loaf; dip pan *very quickly* in and out of hot water. Cover with a chilled serving plate; turn upside down; lift off pan. Garnish with small crisp lettuce leaves, if you wish. Cut in thin slices; serve with crackers.

658

Salmon Mousse in Aspic
Makes 12 servings

2 envelopes unflavored gelatin
2 cans (about 13 ounces each) consommé madrilène
½ cup dry white wine
2 cans (1 pound each) salmon
¼ cup mayonnaise or salad dressing
¼ cup cream for whipping

1 Soften gelatin in 1 can of the madrilène in a medium-size saucepan. Heat, stirring constantly, until gelatin dissolves; remove from heat. Stir in remaining 1 can madrilène.
2 Measure out ½ cup of the mixture and set aside. Stir wine into remaining mixture in saucepan.
3 Drain salmon; bone and flake into a large bowl. Beat in the ½ cup gelatin mixture and mayonnaise or salad dressing. Beat cream until stiff in a small bowl; fold into salmon mixture. Chill while preparing mold.
4 Place a 6-cup fish-shape mold in a large pan of ice and water; let stand 5 minutes; pour in gelatin-wine mixture. Chill 20 minutes, or until gelatin forms a thin coat on bottom and sides of mold; pour off unset gelatin mixture into a bowl.
5 Spoon salmon mixture over layer in mold, spreading to within ½ inch of sides of mold; chill until softly set.
6 Spoon remaining gelatin mixture back into mold around salmon and on top; remove mold from ice and water. Chill in refrigerator at least 6 hours, or until firm.
7 When ready to serve, run a sharp-tip thin-blade knife around top of salad; dip mold *very quickly* in and out of hot water. Cover with a chilled serving plate; turn upside down; lift off mold. Garnish with cucumber cups filled with twists of lemon rind and mayonnaise or salad dressing, and chicory or curly endive, if you wish.

Scandinavian Appetizer Tray
Makes 12 servings

6 medium-size cucumbers
1½ cups cider vinegar
½ cup water
½ cup sugar
1 teaspoon salt
¼ teaspoon white pepper
6 tablespoons chopped fresh dill
  OR: 1 tablespoon dillweed
2 jars (8 ounces each) herring in wine sauce
2 jars (1 pound each) sliced pickled beets
1 medium-size onion, peeled, sliced, and separated into rings

1 Pare cucumbers and slice very thin; place in a medium-size bowl.

2 Combine vinegar, water, sugar, salt, and pepper in a small bowl; stir until sugar dissolves. Pour over cucumber slices; sprinkle with dill. Chill at least 2 hours to season.

3 When ready to serve, drain liquids from cucumbers, herring, and beets. Spoon cucumbers into a shallow serving dish; place in the center of a large serving tray. Arrange herring and beets in sections around cucumbers. Garnish beets with onion rings, and cucumbers and herring with sprigs of fresh dill, if you wish.

Turkey-Ham Galantine
Makes 12 servings

2 packaged frozen boneless turkey-ham roasts, weighing 2 pounds each
2 envelopes unflavored gelatin
½ cup light cream or table cream
4 tablespoons (½ stick) butter or margarine
2 tablespoons all-purpose flour
½ teaspoon salt
3 cups chicken broth (from two 14-ounce cans)
2 hard-cooked egg yolks
  Carrot slices
  Parsley sprigs

1 Two days before your party, roast frozen turkey-ham roasts in their foil packages, following label directions. Remove from packages; cool; wrap in foil or transparent wrap; chill.

2 One day before your party, sprinkle 1 envelope of the gelatin over cream in a small bowl; let stand several minutes to soften gelatin.

3 Melt 2 tablespoons of the butter or margarine in a medium-size saucepan; stir in flour, salt, and 1 cup of the chicken broth. Cook, stirring constantly, until mixture thickens and boils 1 minute; stir in gelatin mixture until dissolved; remove from heat. Chill until as thick as unbeaten egg white.

4 Place turkey-ham roasts on a wire rack set in a jelly-roll pan. Spoon part of the thickened gelatin mixture over roasts to coat; chill until set. Repeat twice more with remaining gelatin mixture, chilling until set between each coat, to make a smooth even coating over roasts.

5 Press egg yolks through a sieve into a small bowl; blend in remaining 2 tablespoons butter or margarine. Press mixture through a cake-decorating set onto top of one roast to form blossoms. Cut petal shapes from carrot slices and arrange with sprigs of parsley around eggs to make flowers and stems.

6 Sprinkle remaining 1 envelope gelatin over remaining 2 cups chicken broth in a small saucepan; heat, stirring constantly, until gelatin dissolves. Chill until as thick as unbeaten egg white. Spoon part over decorations on roast to coat well. Remove both roasts to a clean tray or plate; chill.

7 Pour remaining gelatin mixture into a pan, 8x8x2; chill several hours, or until firm.

8 When ready to serve, place decorated roast on a large serving plate; slice second roast and arrange slices at side. Cut gelatin mixture in pan into very tiny cubes; spoon evenly around meat on plate.

Fish Balls with Parsley Sauce
Makes 12 servings

2 packages (1 pound each) frozen haddock fillets
1 cup cracker meal (from an about-10-ounce package)
2 teaspoons salt
¼ teaspoon white pepper
1½ cups light cream or table cream
  PARSLEY SAUCE (recipe follows)
  Paprika

1 Thaw haddock just enough to cut into chunks with a heavy knife. Put through a food grinder twice, using a fine blade. Place in a large bowl.

2 Beat in cracker meal, salt, pepper, and cream until mixture is smooth.

3 Moisten hands; shape mixture into 1-inch balls.

4 Half-fill a large frying pan with water; heat to boiling. Drop fish balls, half at a time, into pan; simmer 10 minutes. Lift out with a slotted spoon;

659

Steaming and savory: Fish Balls with Parsley Sauce.

drain on paper toweling. Place in a serving dish; keep warm until all are cooked.

5 Pour PARSLEY SAUCE over fish balls; sprinkle with paprika.

PARSLEY SAUCE—Melt 6 tablespoons (¾ stick) butter or margarine in a large saucepan. Stir in ⅓ cup sifted all-purpose flour, 1 teaspoon salt, ⅛ teaspoon nutmeg, and a dash of white pepper; cook, stirring constantly, until bubbly. Stir in 2½ cups light cream or table cream; continue cooking and stirring until sauce thickens and boils 1 minute. Just before serving, stir in ¼ cup chopped parsley.

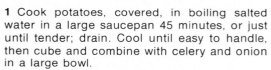

Dilled Potato-Salad Platter
Makes 12 servings

    5 pounds medium-size potatoes
    2 cups chopped celery
    1 medium-size onion, chopped (½ cup)
    2 cups mayonnaise or salad dressing
    ½ cup milk
    2 tablespoons dill seeds, crushed
    1 teaspoon salt
      Dash of pepper
      Boston lettuce
      STUFFED EGGS (recipe follows)
    1 tablespoon chopped parsley

1 Cook potatoes, covered, in boiling salted water in a large saucepan 45 minutes, or just until tender; drain. Cool until easy to handle, then cube and combine with celery and onion in a large bowl.
2 Blend mayonnaise or salad dressing, milk, dill seeds, salt, and pepper in a small bowl; fold into potato mixture.
3 Spoon into a 12-cup bowl; press down lightly with back of spoon to make top even; cover. Chill several hours.
4 When ready to serve, loosen salad around edge with a thin-blade knife; invert onto a serving plate; lift off bowl. Frame salad with lettuce; arrange STUFFED EGGS around edge. Sprinkle salad with parsley and garnish with shredded green-onion tops, if you wish.

STUFFED EGGS—Hard-cook 12 eggs; shell. Cut each in half lengthwise; scoop out yolks into a medium-size bowl; mash well. Stir in ½ cup mayonnaise or salad dressing and 1 tablespoon prepared mustard. Pile back into whites. Top each with red caviar (from a 4-ounce jar).

660

Sweet-Sour Brown Beans
Makes 12 servings

    2 pounds dried Swedish brown beans
    10 cups water

Sweet-Sour Brown Beans add zip to Smorgasbord.

    3 teaspoons salt
    ½ cup firmly packed brown sugar
    ½ cup cider vinegar
      Sliced green onions

1 Wash beans and sort; combine with water in a kettle.
2 Heat to boiling; cook 2 minutes; cover. Remove from heat; let stand 1 hour.
3 Stir in salt and just enough water, if needed, to cover beans. Heat to boiling; simmer 1½ hours, or until beans are tender. (If needed during cooking, add additional water.)
4 Stir in brown sugar and vinegar; heat 10 minutes to blend flavors. Spoon into a heated serving bowl; sprinkle with sliced green onions.
Note—If you cannot find Swedish brown beans in your supermarket, substitute dried red kidney beans.

Caraway Cabbage Toss
Makes 12 servings

    1 medium-size head cabbage
    ⅔ cup vegetable oil
    ⅓ cup vinegar
    1 tablespoon caraway seeds
    1 teaspoon sugar

½ teaspoon salt
Dash of pepper
3 medium-size apples
Large romaine leaves

1 Trim outer leaves from cabbage; quarter head and cut out core. Shred cabbage fine. (There will be about 9 cups.) Place in a large bowl.
2 Combine vegetable oil, vinegar, caraway seeds, sugar, salt, and pepper in a jar with a tight-fitting lid; shake well to mix. Pour over cabbage; toss lightly; cover. Chill several hours.
3 When ready to serve, quarter apples; core; slice thin crosswise. Set aside a few slices for garnish; toss remainder with cabbage mixture. Spoon into a romaine-lined salad bowl; overlap remaining apple slices on top.

Swedish Apple Cake
Bake at 350° for 30 minutes. Makes 12 servings

1 package (6 ounces) zwieback
½ cup (1 stick) butter or margarine, melted
2 teaspoons grated lemon rind
2 jars or cans (15 or 16 ounces each) apple-sauce
1 package (about 3 ounces) vanilla pudding and pie filling mix
3 cups milk
2 teaspoons vanilla
1 cup cream for whipping

1 Crush zwieback fine. (There will be about 2½ cups.) Toss with melted butter or margarine in a large bowl. Measure out 1 cup of the mixture and press into a baking dish, 9x9x2.
2 Stir lemon rind into applesauce in a me-dium-size bowl; spread half over crumb layer in pan. Sprinkle with half of the remaining crumb mixture; spread with remaining applesauce mixture; sprinkle with remaining crumb mixture.
3 Bake in moderate oven (350°) 30 minutes, or until firm and golden. Cool in dish on wire rack.
4 Several hours before serving, prepare pud-ding mix with milk, following label directions; stir in vanilla; chill.
5 Just before serving, beat cream until stiff in a medium-size bowl. Cut cake into squares; place on rimmed serving plates. Spoon custard sauce around cake; top with whipped cream. Garnish each with a small spoonful of red cur-rant jelly, if you wish.

Lingonberry Torte
Bake at 350° for 10 minutes, then at 325° for 30 minutes. Makes one 9-inch 2-layer torte

3 squares unsweetened chocolate
1 cup milk
1 cup sifted all-purpose flour
2½ teaspoons baking powder
½ teaspoon salt
4 whole eggs
1 egg yolk
1⅓ cups sugar
1½ teaspoons almond extract
LINGONBERRY JAM (recipe follows)
COFFEE FROSTING (recipe follows)

1 Melt chocolate in milk in top of a double boiler over hot water; remove from heat; cool.
2 Sift flour, baking powder, and salt onto wax paper.
3 Beat egg and egg yolk until fluffy-light in a medium-size bowl; slowly beat in sugar until creamy-thick. Stir in almond extract and choco-late mixture; fold in flour mixture. Pour into 2 greased 9x1½-inch layer-cake pans, dividing evenly.
4 Bake in moderate oven (350°) 10 minutes. Lower oven temperature to slow (325°). Bake 30 minutes longer, or until a wooden pick in-serted in center comes out clean.
5 Cool layers in pans on wire racks 5 minutes.

Loosen around edges with a knife; turn out; cool completely.
6 Spread LINGONBERRY JAM over one layer; place on a serving plate; top with second layer. Frost side and top of torte with COFFEE FROSTING, spreading evenly.

LIGONBERRY JAM—Combine 1 jar (about 15 ounces) ligonberries with ½ cup sugar in a small saucepan. Heat, stirring constantly, to boiling, then cook, stirring constantly, about 5 minutes, or until mixture is very thick. Cool.

COFFEE FROSTING—Sift 1 package (1 pound) 10X (confectioners' powdered) sugar onto wax paper. Cream ½ cup (1 stick) butter or marga-rine with half of the sugar until fluffy-light in a medium-size bowl. Combine 1 tablespoon instant coffee, 1 teaspoon vanilla, and 3 table-spoons milk in a cup; slowly beat into butter mixture, adding alternately with remaining sugar, until frosting is smooth and easy to spread. Makes enough to frost two 9-inch layers.

661

AN ALFRESCO FEAST FOR 16

Dip-and-Chip Tray
Meat Ball Outriggers/Honolulu Heroes
Chicken Steamers
Mauna Loa Cream Tower
Hilo Fruits/Islands Sundae Sauce
Kona Cream
Fruit Punch/Brownie Rounds

Chicken Steamers
They're stacked three layers high with a cool avocado spread and fruited meat salad as the fillings.
Makes 16 servings

1 broiler-fryer, weighing about 2½ pounds
1 cup water
1½ teaspoons salt
Few celery tops
1 can (about 9 ounces) pineapple tidbits
½ cup halved green grapes
1 cup mayonnaise or salad dressing
1 medium-size firm ripe avocado
6 slices crisp bacon, crumbled
Few drops liquid red pepper seasoning
2 loaves Italian bread

1 Combine chicken with water, 1 teaspoon of the salt, and celery tops in a large saucepan; heat to boiling; cover. Simmer 1 hour, or until tender.
2 Remove from broth and cool until easy to handle; strain broth and chill for soup or gravy. Pull skin from chicken and take meat from bones; dice. (There should be about 2 cups.) Place in a medium-size bowl.
3 Drain syrup from pineapple into a cup. Add pineapple and grapes to chicken. Blend 2 tablespoons of the syrup with ½ cup of the mayonnaise or salad dressing and remaining ½ teaspoon salt in a small bowl; fold into chicken mixture. Chill.
4 Halve avocado; pit and peel. Mash in a small bowl; stir in crumbled bacon, ¼ cup of the remaining mayonnaise or salad dressing, and red pepper seasoning. (Fix avocado mixture no longer than an hour ahead so that it keeps its bright color.)

662

Way to wow 16 friends: a Hawaii-style Luau featuring Meat Ball Outriggers, Honolulu Heroes and rainbow-colored, tall, frosty Mauna Loa Cream Tower.

5 Cut each loaf of bread lengthwise into 3 even slices; spread with remaining ¼ cup mayonnaise or salad dressing.
6 Spread avocado mixture on bottom slices and chicken salad on middle slices; stack back in shape; cover with top slices. Cut each sandwich crosswise into 8 thick slices.

Meat Ball Outriggers

Hollow loaves of bread, then heap with saucy ground-beef balls. Be sure to set out knives and forks for everyone.
Makes 16 servings

4 loaves Italian bread
3 pounds ground beef
2 eggs, slightly beaten
2 tablespoons instant minced onion
3 teaspoons salt
1 teaspoon paprika
½ cup milk
2 tablespoons vegetable oil
2 tablespoons all-purpose flour
1 bottle (12 ounces) chili sauce
1 cup water
1 tablespoon light brown sugar
1 teaspoon dry mustard
Butter or margarine

1 Cut a ½-inch-thick slice from top of each loaf of bread; cut out inside to leave a ½-inch-thick boat-shape shell. Crumble enough of the insides to measure 2½ cups; save remaining with top slices to turn into croutons for another day. Cover loaves to keep them from drying out.
2 Combine ground beef, the 2½ cups bread crumbs, eggs, onion, salt, paprika, and milk in a large bowl; mix lightly until well-blended. Shape into tiny balls, using 1 tablespoon for each. (There should be about 110 meat balls.)
3 Brown, part at a time, in vegetable oil in a large frying pan; remove with a slotted spoon to a large bowl.
4 Stir flour into drippings in frying pan; cook, stirring constantly, just until bubbly. Stir in chili sauce and water; continue cooking and stirring, scraping cooked-on juices from bottom and side of pan, until sauce thickens and boils 1 minute. Stir in brown sugar and mustard.
5 Place meat balls in sauce; cover. Simmer 30 minutes.
6 Spread hollows of loaves with butter or margarine; heat in slow oven (325°) 10 minutes.
7 Spoon about 2 cups of the meat balls and sauce into each. Cut into quarters to eat with a knife and fork.

664

Honolulu Heroes

As American as our 50th state! Filling can be cold cuts and sliced cheeses of your choice, but pile them high.
Makes 16 servings

2 loaves Italian bread
Butter or margarine
3 packages (6 ounces each) sliced cold cuts
1 package (8 ounces) sliced Swiss cheese
1 package (8 ounces) sliced process American cheese
Boston lettuce
3 medium-size tomatoes, sliced thin
4 hard-cooked eggs, shelled and sliced
1 envelope (2 to a package) onion-soup mix
1 cup (8-ounce carton) dairy sour cream
½ cup milk

1 Split loaves of bread; spread with butter or margarine.
2 Fold half of the cold meat slices and roll remaining; roll Swiss cheese slices; fold American cheese slices. (Cheese rolls perfectly without cracking if warmed to room temperature first.)
3 Layer meat, lettuce, American cheese, tomato slices, egg slices, Swiss cheese, and remaining meat, dividing evenly, onto bottom halves of bread.
4 Blend onion-soup mix with sour cream and milk in a small bowl; spoon part over filling on sandwiches; cover with tops of loaves. Trim with tiny sprigs of parsley held in place with fancy wooden picks. To serve sandwich, cut each into 8 thick slices, serve remaining dressing separately.

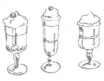

Mauna Loa Cream Tower

Big and showy, it calls for three flavors of packaged ice cream and sherbet plus a simple molding trick.
Makes 16 servings

1 pint raspberry sherbet
2 pints orange sherbet
½ gallon vanilla ice cream

1 Pack raspberry sherbet into the bottom of a deep 12-cup mold; freeze until firm.
2 Repeat with orange sherbet, then vanilla ice cream; cover. Freeze until serving time.
3 When ready to serve, dip mold very quickly in and out of a pan of hot water; invert onto

a large serving plate; lift off mold. Frame ice cream with BROWNIE ROUNDS (recipe follows) and your choice of sundae sauces.

●

Hilo Fruits
Pineapple, papaya, and bananas blend with ginger for a different ice-cream topper.
Makes 4 cups

1 can (about 14 ounces) frozen pineapple chunks, thawed
1 jar (14 ounces) papaya, drained and cubed
2 tablespoons chopped crystallized or pre-served ginger
2 medium-size firm ripe bananas

1 Combine pineapple and syrup, papaya, and ginger in a medium-size bowl; chill at least a half hour to season.
2 Just before serving, peel bananas and slice; fold into fruit mixture. Serve in small bowls to spoon over ice cream.

●

Islands Sundae Sauce
Royally red and lightly spiced! Just see how easily it goes together with frozen punch.
Makes 2½ cups

2 cans (16 ounces each) frozen concentrate for juicy red Hawaiian punch
2 cups white corn syrup
½ cup water
1 three-inch piece stick cinnamon

1 Combine concentrate for punch, corn syrup, water, and cinnamon in a large heavy saucepan; heat slowly, stirring constantly, to boiling, then cook 15 minutes, or until slightly thickened.
2 Remove cinnamon stick. Cool, then chill if made ahead. (For best flavor and easy spoon-ing, remove sauce from refrigerator at least a half hour before serving.) Serve in small bowls to spoon over ice cream.

●

Kona Cream
This rich sauce owes its candylike flavor to brown sugar and coffee. Recipe makes lots, but it's a good keeper.
Makes 4 cups

1½ cups firmly packed light brown sugar
2 tablespoons instant coffee powder
Dash of salt
1 cup water
2 cans (about 15 ounces each) sweetened condensed milk (not evaporated)
2 teaspoons rum flavoring or extract

1 Combine brown sugar, instant coffee, salt, and water in a medium-size saucepan.
2 Heat, stirring constantly, to boiling, then cook, without stirring, to 230° on a candy ther-mometer. (A teaspoon of syrup will spin a thread when dropped from spoon.) Remove from heat.
3 Stir hot syrup into condensed milk in a me-dium-size bowl; stir in rum flavoring or extract. Chill. Serve in small bowls to spoon over ice cream.

●

Brownie Rounds
What could be more popular? And it's fun to tint the frosting.
Bake at 350° for 10 minutes. Makes 4 dozen

1 package (about 1 pound) brownie mix
2 eggs
2 tablespoons water
1 can (1 pound, 5 ounces) vanilla frosting
Yellow and green food colorings

1 Combine brownie mix, eggs, and water in a medium-size bowl; beat until blended.
2 Drop by teaspoonfuls, 2 inches apart, on greased cookie sheets.
3 Bake in moderate oven (350°) 10 minutes, or until firm. Cool on cookie sheets 1 minute, then remove to wire racks; cool completely.
4 Divide frosting into 2 small bowls; tint one pale yellow and the other green with food color-ings. Spread each color on half of the cookies. Sprinkle with decorating sequins and flowers, if you wish.

A COLLECTION OF CROWD PLEASERS

One great dish can make the party—and it needn't be a purse-emptier. On a value-for-money basis, the recipes included here prove that quality need not be sacrificed for quantity. Creativity is the magic ingredient.

Glazed Pork Shoulder
Roast at 375° for 30 minutes. Makes 10 to 12 servings

1 cook-before-eating smoked pork picnic shoulder (about 5 pounds)
Water
1 tablespoon mixed pickling spices

665

Guaranteed to serve a crowd, guaranteed to impress: Glazed Pork Shoulder, a whopping dish of Cassoulet for a Crowd and Party Meat Loaf wrapped Wellington-style in pastry.

1 cup firmly packed brown sugar
1 cup apple juice
¼ teaspoon ground cloves
½ cup chopped parsley

1 Place picnic shoulder in a kettle; add cold water to cover; add pickling spices.
2 Heat slowly to boiling; reduce heat; cover. Simmer 2½ hours, or until meat is tender when pierced with a two-tined fork. Remove from heat; allow meat to cool in liquid at least 30 minutes.
3 Place picnic shoulder in a shallow roasting pan. Cut skin from top of meat; score fat.
4 To make sauce: Combine brown sugar, apple juice, and cloves in a small saucepan. Heat to boiling; reduce heat; simmer 5 minutes. Remove sauce from heat; stir in chopped parsley. Brush part of sauce over meat.
5 Roast in moderate oven (375°), basting several times with part of sauce, 30 minutes, or until well glazed.
6 Pass remaining sauce separately. Serve with baked sweet potatoes and spiced pear halves, if you wish.

Bountiful Beef Stew
Makes 12 servings

4 pounds boneless beef chuck or round
1 can (about 1 pound) Italian tomatoes, drained
⅓ cup red wine vinegar
2 tablespoons olive oil or vegetable oil
2 tablespoons chopped parsley
3 teaspoons salt
2 teaspoons leaf oregano, crumbled
1½ teaspoons garlic powder
1 teaspoon leaf basil, crumbled
¼ teaspoon pepper
Hot cooked rice

1 Trim all fat from beef; cut into 1½-inch cubes.
2 Place beef, tomatoes, vinegar, oil, parsley, salt, oregano, garlic powder, basil, and pepper in a large heavy saucepan.
3 Heat slowly to boiling; reduce heat; cover. Simmer 2 hours, or until meat is tender when pierced with a two-tined fork. Serve with hot cooked rice.

Cassoulet for a Crowd
Bake at 350° for 1½ hours. Makes 12 to 16 servings

1 frozen turkey (about 6 pounds), thawed
2 ham hocks (about 1 pound each)

8 cups water
1 cup grated carrot (2 medium-size)
2 large onions, chopped (2 cups)
3 teaspoons salt
2 cloves of garlic, sliced
2 bay leaves
1 teaspoon leaf thyme, crumbled
3 sprigs of parsley
4 cups dried large lima beans (from a 2-pound bag)

1 Place turkey with giblets and ham hocks in a kettle or Dutch oven. Add water, carrot, onion, and salt.
2 Place garlic, bay leaves, thyme, and parsley sprigs in a piece of cheesecloth and tie with a string. Push under liquid in kettle.
3 Heat slowly to boiling; reduce heat; cover. Simmer 1 hour, or until turkey is tender. Discard herb bag. Place meats, giblets and liquid in one or two large bowls and chill. (Overnight is best.)
4 Remove meats and giblets from liquid; reserve liquid. Take skin, fat, and bones from turkey and ham; cut meats and giblets into small pieces; reserve in refrigerator.
5 Pick over beans; combine with reserved broth in a kettle; heat to boiling and boil 2 minutes; cover. Remove from heat; let stand 1 hour.
6 Heat beans to boiling again; reduce heat; cover. Simmer 2 hours, or until beans are tender. Add reserved meats and giblets; toss lightly to mix. Spoon into a 16-cup baking dish or two 8-cup baking dishes.
7 Bake in moderate oven (350°) 1½ hours, or until bubbly in center. Sprinkle with chopped parsley, if you wish.

Party Meat Loaf
Bake at 375° for 1 hour, then at 425° for 15 minutes. Makes 12 servings

3 pounds meat-loaf mixture (ground beef, pork and veal)
2 cups fresh white bread crumbs (4 slices)
1 cup (4 ounces) shredded Swiss cheese
½ cup finely chopped dill pickle
3 tablespoons dill pickle juice
3 teaspoons salt
¼ teaspoon pepper
1 tall (14½ ounces) can evaporated milk
3 eggs
2 cups sifted all-purpose flour
⅔ cup vegetable shortening

1 Combine meat-loaf mixture, bread crumbs, cheese, dill pickle and juice, 2 teaspoons of the salt, pepper, and 1⅓ cups of the evaporated milk in a large bowl. (Reserve remaining salt and milk for pastry.) Beat eggs in a small bowl. (Reserve 2 tablespoons of the beaten egg for pastry.) Add remaining beaten egg to meat mixture.

2 Mix meat mixture (using fingers is best) until very smooth, and almost pastelike in consistency. Shape into a loaf, 12x5x2, in a jelly-roll pan.

3 Bake in moderate oven (375°) 1 hour, or until top is a rich brown. Cool meat loaf completely in pan on wire rack.

4 Sift flour and remaining 1 teaspoon salt into a medium-size bowl; cut in shortening with a pastry blender until mixture is crumbly. Sprinkle with remaining ⅓ cup evaporated milk, one tablespoon at a time. Mix lightly with a fork just until pastry holds together and leaves side of bowl clean.

5 Roll out pastry to a 15-inch square on a lightly floured pastry cloth. Lay pastry over rolling pin and transfer to a large cookie sheet.

6 Loosen meat loaf on pan and transfer, with two spatulas, to center of pastry. (If making gravy, reserve pan drippings.) Bring pastry up to cover meat at center top. Trim off excess

pastry and reserve. Press pastry firmly to seal at center of loaf and at ends.

7 Make an egg wash by combining reserved beaten egg and 2 tablespoons of water in a cup; brush part over pastry. Roll pastry trimmings and cut with tiny fancy cutters. Arrange in a pattern on loaf and brush with part of the remaining egg wash.

8 Bake in hot oven (425°) brushing once with remaining egg wash, 15 minutes, or until pastry is golden. Serve hot or cold. Garnish with tomato wedges and parsley sprigs, if you wish.

If meat loaf is to be served hot, you may wish to serve this gravy with it.

RICH PAN GRAVY—Add 3 cups water to pan in which the meat loaf was baked. Bring to bubbling over medium heat, scraping to loosen baked-on juices. Strain into a small saucepan. Combine 4 tablespoons flour and ½ cup cold water to make a smooth paste in a cup. Heat liquid in saucepan to bubbling; stir in flour mixture; continue cooking and stirring until gravy thickens and bubbles 1 minute. Season with bottled gravy coloring, and salt and pepper to taste. Makes about 3½ cups.

A beautiful, budget-minded way to cope with a crowd is to simmer a giant cauldron of your favorite stew.

COOKING FOR

COOKING FOR JUST TWO:
SOME AMOUNTS OF FOOD RECOMMENDED,
HALF A DOZEN DINNERS FOR TWO

Cooking for two persons is neither confining nor complicated once you learn a few tricks. It's pointless, for example, to roast a mini-roast—it will merely toughen and dry. Far better to buy a medium-size roast, say four or five pounds, and to plan ingenious ways of using up the leftovers *before* you pop the roast into the oven. Leg of lamb makes luscious curry; roast beef takes to Shepherd's Pie; ham to dozens of casseroles (you'll find them elsewhere in the FAMILY CIRCLE ILLUSTRATED LIBRARY OF COOKING as well as a number of other creative ways of using up leftovers).

Foods in individual-size portions, of course, simplify cooking for two: small steaks, chops and such vegetables as artichokes, potatoes and tomatoes. A nifty trick with other vegetables—green peas, for example, green beans or limas—is to shell or snap several pounds at once, to pop them into plastic bags and refrigerate or freeze for future use so that you can pull out a cup or so at a time. It's also wise to make up salad dressings, sauces and desserts in quantities for two or more meals. Takes no more time to make a lot than to make a little. And it pays to grate several cups of cheese at a time or to roll several cups of dry bread crumbs so that they're ready and waiting in the refrigerator whenever you need them to scatter over a casserole or slip into a recipe.

Think of your refrigerator and freezer as a bank, depositing there hamburgers shaped and ready to cook, tomatoey sauces, leftover meats and vegetables. Then withdraw them as needed, team them together, try them in new ways. You'll soon have an impressive repertoire of recipes built for two.

In the pages that follow, you will find a list of foods in amounts to serve two persons to simplify marketing, also half a dozen menus (with recipes) that will feed two heartily, happily.

SOME AMOUNTS OF FOOD RECOMMENDED FOR TWO PEOPLE

Hearty, always a hit and kind to the budget: sausages of every shape and flavor. Cook them for big "do's."

MEATS:	QUANTITY
Steaks: Rib, Club, Skirt, Filet Mignon	2 of the thickness you like
T-Bone, Sirloin, Porterhouse	1 cut about 1-inch thick
Flank	1 (for 2 meals)
Ham Steak	1 center-cut slice ½-to ¾-inch thick
Chops: Lamb and Pork Rib and Loin	2 to 4 of thickness you like
Veal	2 of thickness you like

COOKING FOR JUST TWO

MEATS:	QUANTITY
Roasts: Beef, Veal, Lamb, Pork Ham	4 pounds (*Note:* Small roasts cook poorly so buy a larger roast and plan for leftovers at time of purchase)
Stew Meat	¾ to 1 pound depending upon heartiness of stew
Short Ribs, Spareribs	1½ to 2 pounds
Veal Cutlets, Scaloppine	¾ to 1 pound
Hamburger Meat	⅔ to ¾ pound

VARIETY, SPECIALTY MEATS:	QUANTITY
Bacon	⅓ pound
Sausage	⅓ to ½ pound
Frankfurters	4
Liver	½ pound
Lamb Kidneys	4
Veal Kidneys	2

POULTRY:	QUANTITY
Broiler-Fryer	1½ to 2 pounds, split, for broiling 2 to 2½ pounds, cut up, for frying
Chicken Breasts	1 to 2 whole, weighing about 12 ounces each, depending upon how simply or lavishly prepared
Drumsticks or Thighs	4
Roasting Chicken	3½ to 4 pounds (enough for 2 meals)
Game Hens	2

SEAFOOD:	QUANTITY
Fish Fillets	¾ pound
Small Whole Fish	2
Fish Steak (salmon, etc.)	¾ pound
Oysters, Clams, Mussels	One dozen
Lobster	2 small (1½ pounds) or 1 large (3 pounds or more)
Lobster Tails	2 large
Shrimp (in the shell)	1 pound
Shrimp (shelled)	½ to ¾ pound
Scallops	½ to ¾ pound
Crabmeat	½ pound

VEGETABLES:	QUANTITY
Artichokes	2 medium-size to large
Asparagus	¾ pound
Beans (green, wax)	½ pound
Beans (limas, in the shell)	1 pound
Beets	2 to 4, depending on size
Broccoli	½ bunch
Brussels Sprouts	1 pound
Cabbage	½ to ¾ pound
Carrots	2 to 3 per person, depending on size; about ½ bunch
Cauliflower	1 small head
Corn-on-the-Cob	4 ears
Corn (Whole Kernel or Cream-Style)	½ to ¾ cup per person
Eggplant	1 small
Lettuce, Other Salad Greens	½ pound
Mushrooms	¼ to ½ pound
Peas (green, in the shell)	¼ to ½ pound
Potatoes (Irish and Sweet)	1 medium size per person; allow 2 to 3 new potatoes per person
Spinach, Collards, Kale, Turnip Greens	1 pound
Summer Squash, Zucchini	2 to 4, depending on size
Winter Squash (Acorn, Butternut,	2 small
Tomatoes	2 medium-size; 8 to 10 cherry tomatoes
Turnips, Rutabaga	1 pound

FRUITS:	QUANTITY
Apples, Bananas, Peaches, Pears, Oranges	2 medium-size
Berries	1 pint
Grapefruit	2 medium-size
Grapes	½ to ¾ pound
Melons	1 small
Pineapple	1 small
Rhubarb	1 pound

MISCELLANEOUS:	QUANTITY
Ice Cream	½ to ⅔ pint
Sherbet, Ices	½ to ¾ pint
Custards, Puddings	½ pint
Eggs	3 to 4 for scrambling

672

Beef Tenderloin Steaks

All America loves beef, especially if it's steak and most especially if it's a succulent-tender sirloin.

Simply glorious, whether cooked for family or feast: a boned and rolled prime ribs of beef, juicily-pink.

Good choice for two people not up to an entire sirloin steak: Top Sirloin.

The beauty of nature's harvest, particularly vegetables plucked in their prime, invariably impresses.

More of nature's bounty by the bushel: garden-fresh greens, beans and tomatoes, carrots, onions and radishes.

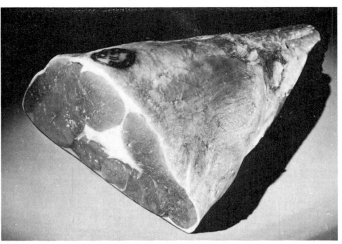

Good choice for a small family, a small but tender and juicy Veal Heel of Round.

Rolled Shoulder of Lamb Roast

Loveliest lamb chops are Loin.

676

Chunks of lamb for stew.

Pork Blade Loin Roast.

Back Ribs, a barbecue favorite.

677

Smoked Ham Slice, center-cut.

Smoked Picnic Shoulder.

Great on the grill—Spareribs.

678

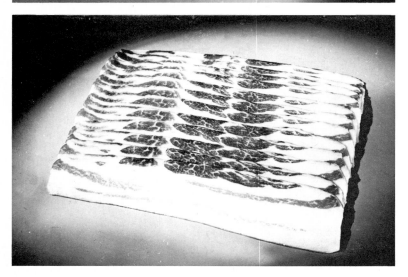

Extra-lean bacon slices.

HALF A DOZEN DINNERS FOR TWO

I
Cape Cod Fish Chowder
Chowder Crackers
Harvest Bowl Salad
Hot Sliced Peaches and Cream
Coffee   Tea

Cape Cod Fish Chowder
With lots of fish, potatoes, corn, and milk, it makes a whole main dish in a bowl.
Makes 2 servings

⅓ cup chopped onion
1½ tablespoons butter or margarine
1 large potato, pared and sliced (1⅓ cups)
½ teaspoon salt
¼ teaspoon leaf basil, crumbled
    Pinch pepper
1¼ cups water
½ pound frozen cod or haddock fillets, partly thawed and cut into cubes
1 can (8 ounces) whole-kernel corn
1 small can evaporated milk (⅔ cup)

1 Sauté onion in butter or margarine until soft in a kettle; add potatoes, salt, basil, pepper, and water; cover. Simmer 15 minutes.
2 Place fish on top of potatoes; cover again. Simmer 15 minutes, or until fish flakes easily and potatoes are tender.
3 Stir in corn and liquid and evaporated milk; cover. Heat just to boiling.
4 Ladle into heated large soup bowls; sprinkle with chopped parsley and pimiento, and serve with chowder crackers.

Harvest Salad Bowl
Perky topknot of sunny carrot garnishes salads of coleslaw and mixed greens.
Makes 2 servings

1 cup shredded cabbage
1 teaspoon sugar
2 tablespoons mayonnaise or salad dressing
1 teaspoon lemon juice
    Pinch salt
    Pinch pepper
1½ cups broken mixed salad greens
½ medium-size carrot, pared and grated

1 Place cabbage in a medium-size bowl; sprinkle with sugar; toss to mix; cover. Chill 30 minutes.
2 Blend mayonnaise or salad dressing, lemon

juice, salt, and pepper in a cup; pour over cabbage; toss to mix well.
3 Divide salad greens evenly among 6 individual salad bowls; spoon cabbage mixture in center; garnish each with a mound of grated carrot.

II
Clam Juice on-the-Rocks
Baked Chicken Parmesan
Hot Fluffy Rice
Skillet Zucchini
Tart Lemon Ice   Macaroons
Coffee   Tea

Baked Chicken Parmesan
An easy and pleasing variation of the beloved Italian veal dish. This time it's chicken that's flavored with piquant Parmesan cheese.
Bake at 425° about 40 minutes. Makes 2 servings

2 tablespoons olive oil
1 chicken breast (about 12 ounces)
½ teaspoon leaf oregano, crumbled
¼ teaspoon salt
    Paprika
1 can (3 or 4 ounces) sliced mushrooms
1 tablespoon grated Parmesan cheese

1 Line a small shallow baking pan with aluminum foil. Pour olive oil into pan. Place in hot oven (425°) to heat, about 5 minutes. Remove pan from oven.
2 Halve chicken breasts and place, skin side down, in hot oil. Sprinkle with half the oregano and salt. Sprinkle lightly with paprika. Return to oven and bake 20 minutes.
3 Turn chicken pieces; sprinkle with remaining oregano and salt, and lightly with paprika. Bake 15 minutes longer or until tender; remove from oven.
4 Spoon drippings in pan over chicken. Pour mushrooms (with their liquid) over chicken; sprinkle with Parmesan cheese; bake 5 minutes longer.

Skillet Zucchini
A top-of-the-range way to fix this colorful vegetable.
Makes 2 servings

3 small zucchini (about ½ pound), washed, trimmed, and sliced thin
1½ tablespoons butter or margarine
½ teaspoon sugar
½ teaspoon salt
¼ teaspoon mixed Italian herbs
⅛ teaspoon pepper

679

1 cup canned tomatoes or 1 large ripe tomato,
   peeled, cored and chopped

1 Sauté zucchini lightly in butter or margarine
5 minutes in medium-size frying pan. Sprinkle
with sugar, salt, Italian herbs, and pepper; pour
tomatoes over; stir gently to blend.
2 Cover; cook over low heat about 10 minutes,
or until zucchini is crisply tender.

III
Stuffed Artichokes Italiano
Herb Baked Scallops
Tossed Green Salad
Garlic Bread Chunks
Fruit Compote   Sponge Cake
Coffee   Tea

Stuffed Artichokes Italiano
Makes 2 servings

1 cup coarse bread crumbs (2 slices)
¼ cup chopped parsley
¼ cup grated Parmesan cheese
1 tablespoon minced onion
½ clove of garlic, minced
½ teaspoon salt
⅛ teaspoon pepper
2 large artichokes
2 tablespoons olive oil

1 Mix bread crumbs, parsley, cheese, onion,
garlic, salt, and pepper in a small bowl.
2 Cut stems from artichokes to make base flat;
trim leaf tips with scissors. Wash artichokes
under running cold water; drain well. Spread
petals slightly with fingers.
3 Spoon stuffing into center and about 1 teaspoon stuffing into spaces between leaves. Tie
each artichoke tightly with clean string; stand
in a medium-size deep saucepan. Drizzle 1 tablespoon olive oil over each; pour in boiling
water to a depth of about an inch; cover.
4 Cook 50 minutes, or until tender when pierced
with a fork; remove strings. Serve hot.
Note—To eat, pull away one leaf at a time (stuffing will cling to leaves) and bite into the succulent titbit at base of each. Then cut out fuzzy
choke and eat the heart.

Herb Baked Scallops
Seafood with an Italian flavor—and so easy
when your oven does the cooking.
Bake at 350° for 25 minutes. Makes 2 hearty
servings

Perfect for two persons, savory Herb Baked Scallops.

1 pound fresh sea scallops
   OR: 1 package (1 pound) frozen sea scallops
3 tablespoons butter or margarine
2 tablespoons chopped parsley
1 teaspoon leaf basil, crumbled
   Salt and pepper

1 Wash fresh scallops under running cold
water; drain. Or thaw frozen ones, following
label directions.
2 Arrange scallops in a shallow baking dish;
dot with butter or margarine; sprinkle with parsley, basil, and salt and pepper.
3 Bake in moderate oven (350°) 5 minutes; stir
to coat scallops well with butter mixture; bake
20 minutes longer, or until tender when pierced
with a fork.

IV
Tomato Juice Cocktail
Dixie Dandy
Braised Endive
Onion-Radish Ring
Rice Pudding
Coffee   Tea

Dixie Dandy
Bake at 300° for 30 minutes. Makes 2 servings

1 cup applesauce
⅛ teaspoon ground ginger
½ can (12 ounces) pork luncheon meat
   Whole cloves
2 boiled sweet potatoes, peeled and sliced
½ cup apricot jam
½ teaspoon dry mustard
1 tablespoon water

1 Mix applesauce and ginger in shallow 4-cup
baking dish.
2 Halve meat lengthwise, then cut each half in
6 squares almost through to bottom; stud
squares with cloves. Place on top of applesauce
in dish. Arrange sliced sweet potatoes around
meat.
3 Combine remaining ingredients in 1-cup
measure; spread mixture evenly over meat and
potatoes.
4 Bake in hot oven (400°) 30 minutes, or until
hot and richly glazed.

Braised Endive
Makes 2 servings

4 small stalks Belgian endive
1 tablespoon lemon juice
½ teaspoon salt
2 tablespoons butter or margarine

681

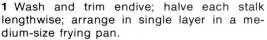

1 Wash and trim endive; halve each stalk lengthwise; arrange in single layer in a medium-size frying pan.
2 Pour in water just to cover spears. (This is important to keep them white during cooking.) Add lemon juice and salt; cover.
3 Heat to boiling, then simmer 10 minutes, or just until tender when pierced with a fork.
4 Lift out stalks carefully with a slotted spoon; place in heated serving dish. Drain liquid from pan.
5 Add butter or margarine and heat slowly, shaking pan continuously, just until butter bubbles up. (Watch closely, so it doesn't turn too brown.) Pour at once over endive.

Onion-Radish-Ring Salad
Makes 2 servings

1 small head of Bibb or Boston lettuce
¼ pound fresh tender spinach, stems removed
½ small sweet red onion, sliced and separated into rings
4 radishes, sliced
¼ cup bottled thin French dressing

1 Tear lettuce and spinach into bite-size pieces; place in salad bowl. Top with onion rings and sliced radishes.
2 Pour French dressing over; toss lightly until greens and vegetables are well coated.

Rice Pudding
It's smooth and creamy, delectably spiced.
Bake at 350° for 40 minutes. Makes 4 servings
(Save the extra 2 to eat another time)

2 cups cooked rice
¼ cup sugar
½ teaspoon cinnamon
2 tablespoons butter or margarine
2 cups milk
½ teaspoon vanilla

1 Combine all ingredients in 6-cup baking dish.
2 Bake in moderate oven (350°) 20 minutes; stir gently. Bake 20 minutes longer, or until creamy-thick. Serve warm or cold, plain or with cream.

682

V
Cheese Tray   Crackers
Chicken Livers Supreme
Buttered Whole Wheat Toast Points
Danish Tomatoes
Bacon Lettuce Bowl
Baked Cinnamon Apples
Coffee   Tea

Chicken Livers Supreme
Rightly named with their supremely delicate flavor. Don't overcook them.
Makes 2 servings

½ pound chicken livers
¼ cup sifted all-purpose flour
½ teaspoon salt
⅛ teaspoon pepper
1½ tablespoons butter or margarine
1 can (3 or 4 ounces) sliced mushrooms
¾ teaspoon Worcestershire sauce

1 Shake chicken livers, a few at a time, in mixture of flour, salt, and pepper in paper bag to coat evenly.
2 Brown in butter or margarine in large heavy frying pan over low heat. Stir in mushrooms and liquid and Worcestershire sauce.
3 Cover loosely; cook slowly 10 minutes, or just until liquid is absorbed.

Danish Tomatoes
Zesty blue cheese dresses this garden favorite.
Makes 2 servings

Blend ¼ cup vegetable oil, 1½ tablespoons cider vinegar, 1 tablespoon crumbled blue cheese, ¼ minced clove of garlic, ¼ teaspoon each sugar and salt, and ⅛ teaspoon pepper together in a small bowl. Pour over 2 sliced tomatoes in a shallow serving dish; sprinkle with 1 teaspoon chopped parsley or chopped watercress. Let stand 30 minutes at room temperature to blend flavors.

Bacon-Lettuce Bowl
Hot zippy bacon-and-vinegar dressing seasons this favorite salad.
Makes 2 servings

¼ head iceberg lettuce
2 slices bacon, cut in ½-inch pieces
1 tablespoon sugar

1 tablespoon cider vinegar
1½ teaspoons water
¼ teaspoon seasoned salt

1 Shred lettuce; place in a salad bowl. (There should be about 2 cups.)
2 Sauté bacon just until crisp in a small frying pan; lift out with slotted spoon and add to lettuce.
3 Pour bacon drippings from pan, then return 2 tablespoonfuls. Stir in remaining ingredients; heat just to boiling.
4 Drizzle over lettuce; toss to mix well.

●

Baked Cinnamon Apples
Bake at 350° for 50 minutes. Makes 2 servings

2 medium-size baking apples
⅔ cup sugar
⅓ cup water
1 two-inch stick cinnamon

1 Wash and core apples; pare halfway to bottom. Stand in deep baking dish.
2 Combine sugar and water in 2-cup measure; pour over apples. Drop in cinnamon stick.
3 Bake in moderate oven (350°), basting often with syrup in dish, 50 minutes, or until apples are tender, but still firm enough to hold their shape.

●

VI
Cranberry Juice Cocktail
Paprika Veal
Confetti Waldorf Salad
Hot Pineapple Sandwich Cake
Coffee　　Tea

Paprika Veal
A favorite European dish made with mild-flavor veal in a rich creamy sauce.
Makes 2 hearty servings

¾ pound lean veal shoulder, cut into 1-inch cubes
3 tablespoons all-purpose flour
3 teaspoons paprika
½ teaspoon salt
2 tablespoons butter or margarine
1 small onion, chopped (⅓ cup)
1 medium-size carrot, pared and grated (about ½ cup)
⅓ cup chopped celery
½ cup water
½ cup dairy sour cream

1 Shake veal cubes, a few at a time, in mixture of flour, 1 teaspoon paprika, and salt in paper

bag to coat evenly. (Save remaining 2 teaspoons paprika for Step 2.)
2 Brown meat in butter or margarine in large heavy frying pan; push to one side. Stir in onion, carrots, celery, and remaining 2 teaspoons paprika; sauté lightly, then mix with meat.
3 Stir in water; cover; cook over low heat 15 to 20 minutes, or until meat is tender.
4 Stir in sour cream; cover again; heat over low heat just until hot.· Spoon over buttered hot noodles.

●

Confetti Waldorf Salad
Everything's cut up like a relish—the kind of crunchy salad you eat and eat.
Makes 2 servings

2 medium-size pared raw carrots, grated (about 1 cup)
1 medium-size apple, diced (about ¾ cup)
½ cup thinly sliced celery
¼ cup sliced radishes
¼ cup coarsely chopped pecans
2 tablespoons mayonnaise
1 teaspoon sugar
¼ teaspoon salt
1½ teaspoons light cream or table cream
1 teaspoon lemon juice

1 Combine carrot, apple, celery, radishes, and pecans in medium-size bowl.
2 Blend remaining ingredients in 1-cup measure; pour over carrot mixture, tossing to mix well. Spoon into serving bowl.

Hot Pineapple Sandwich Cake
Pound-cake slices are your starter for this double-quick dessert.
Bake at 450° for 10 minutes. Makes 4 servings

2 slices frozen pound cake, cut ½ inch thick (from an about-12-ounce package)
½ cup crushed pineapple, well drained (from a 9-ounce can)
1 tablespoon butter or margarine
2 tablespoons brown sugar

1 Place pound cake slices on a cookie sheet; spread with pineapple.
2 Blend butter or margarine into brown sugar with a fork in measuring cup; sprinkle over pineapple.
3 Bake in very hot oven (450°) 10 minutes, or until topping is bubbly-hot.
4 Serve warm, plain or with whipped cream, if you wish.

COOKING ON LOCATION

COOKING ON LOCATION:
GALLEY SUPPERS, MEALS FOR
CAMPERS, MORE
MAIN DISHES TO COOK OUT
OR CARRY, CHECKLIST
FOR CAMPERS AND ALFRESCO CHEFS

With America on an ecology kick, the back-to-nature urge is stronger than ever. Sales of camping equipment have skyrocketed in the past year or two and so many families are answering the call of the wild that conditions at favorite campsites are approaching those of super-crowded cities.

Still, it *is* possible "to split," to wrap oneself in a fir forest, to find a deserted shore or secluded lake within easy driving or boating distance of most large American cities.

Camping today is hardly roughing it. Nor is cooking over a campfire—chances are, the cook takes his own campstove with him (see Outfitting the Alfresco Chef at the end of this section).

Galley slaves have been unfettered, too, because the modern boat galley is as efficient and, in many instances, as elegant as the home kitchen. What all of this means, of course, is that outdoor meals have a decidedly more sophisticated flavor than in days past. As proof, we offer a selection of menus and recipes for both boat galleys and backwoods.

Today's portable campstoves make it possible to cook gourmet fare on the beach or in the back woods.

GALLEY SUPPERS

MARINER'S BUFFET
Shrimp Bites
Drumstick Bake
Seaway Salad Bowl
Toasted Onion Sticks
Pineapple Boats with Nutmeg Cream
Lemon-Mint Iced Tea

Shrimp Bites
Makes 6 servings, 2 each

⅓ cup prepared sandwich spread
2 teaspoons catsup
12 toasted plain crackers or Melba rounds
Chicory or curly endive
1 can (5 ounces) shrimps, drained and rinsed

1 Blend sandwich spread and catsup in a cup; spread on crackers, using about a rounded teaspoonful for each.
2 Top each with a piece of chicory and a shrimp; place on a small serving tray. Garnish with several radish roses, carrot curls, or olives, if you wish.

Good travelers, good grillables: burgers and tomatoes.

Drumstick Bake
Bake at 425° for 50 minutes. Makes 6 servings

½ cup (1 stick) butter or margarine
1 package (5 ounces) barbecue-flavor potato chips
⅓ cup evaporated milk
12 chicken drumsticks
2 cans (15 ounces each) macaroni with cheese sauce
1 can (about 15 ounces) spaghetti with tomato sauce
1 tablespoon instant minced onion
1 large tomato, cut in 6 wedges

1 Melt butter or margarine in a large shallow baking pan.

2 Crush potato chips coarsely. (Tip: Leave chips in bag and simply squeeze it with your hands.) Slit bag; spread open.
3 Pour milk into a shallow dish. Dip drumsticks, 1 at a time, into milk, then roll in potato chips to coat well all over; place in a single layer in butter in pan.
4 Bake in hot oven (425°) 25 minutes; spoon drippings in pan over chicken. Bake 25 minutes longer, or until tender.
5 While chicken bakes, mix macaroni, spaghetti, and onion in a 12-cup baking dish; cover. Heat in oven with chicken 20 minutes, or until bubbly.
6 To serve, arrange drumsticks, spoke fashion, over macaroni mixture in dish; place tomato wedges in a circle in center. Garnish with parsley, if you wish.
Note—If your boat does not have an oven, cook chicken and heat macaroni mixture on top of the range. Then put together, casserole style, for serving, if you wish.

Seaway Salad Bowl
Makes 6 servings

1 medium-size head romaine, broken in bite-size pieces
1 large sweet red pepper, halved, seeded, and cut in thin strips
1 small head chicory or curly endive, separated into leaves
1 large sweet onion, peeled, sliced thin, and separated into rings
Bottled Italian salad dressing

1 Layer romaine, red pepper, chicory, and onion rings into a salad bowl.
2 Just before serving, drizzle with about ¼ cup Italian dressing; toss lightly to mix.

Toasted Onion Sticks
Bake at 425° for 10 minutes. Makes 6 servings, 2 each

1 large loaf French bread
½ cup (1 stick) butter or margarine
1 envelope (2 packets) toasted onion dip mix

1 Split bread in half lengthwise and crosswise; cut each quarter into 3 long sticks.
2 Blend butter or margarine and dip mix in a small bowl; spread on cut sides of bread. Place on a large cookie sheet.
3 Bake in hot oven (425°) 10 minutes, or until toasted. Serve hot.

Pineapple Boats with Nutmeg Cream
Makes 6 servings

1 large fresh pineapple
5 large red plums, quartered and pitted
2 cups (1 pint) strawberries, washed and hulled
1 carton (16 ounces) dairy sour cream (2 cups)
¼ cup firmly packed brown sugar
½ teaspoon ground nutmeg

1 Halve pineapple lengthwise through leafy crown with a heavy sharp knife, then cut each half into 3 wedges. Trim core from each wedge.
2 Working with one wedge at a time, loosen fruit from rind but leave in place, then cut crosswise into 6 slices. Push slices alternately to back and front; fill spaces in half of the wedges with plum quarters and in remainder with strawberries.
3 Blend sour cream with brown sugar and nutmeg in a small bowl. Serve as a sauce or dip with fruit.

Lemon-Mint Iced Tea
Makes 6 servings

1 envelope (about 2 ounces) lemon-flavor iced tea mix
1 envelope (about 2 ounces) mint-flavor iced tea mix
4 cups water
Ice cubes

1 Dissolve iced tea mixes in water in a large pitcher.
2 Pour over ice in 6 tall glasses. Garnish each with a slice of fresh lemon, if you wish.

●

DOCKSIDE EASY
Tomato Tango
Pork Chow Mein
Captain's Cake
Hot Tea

For a feast afloat, try Drumstick Bake, Toasted Onion Sticks and Pineapple Boats with Nutmeg Cream.

Tomato Tango
Makes 4 servings, 1 cup each

2 cans (16 ounces each) tomato-clam cocktail
1 tablespoon lemon juice
4 drops liquid red pepper seasoning
½ teaspoon celery salt

1 Combine all ingredients in a large pitcher; stir well to mix. Chill at least an hour to blend flavors.
2 Pour into cups or glasses; garnish each with a wedge of lemon, if you wish.

Pork Chow Mein
Makes 4 generous servings

1 cup thinly sliced celery
3 tablespoons vegetable oil
1 can (5 ounces) water chestnuts, drained and sliced
1 divider-pack can (2 pounds, 11 ounces) mushroom chow mein
1 tablespoon soy sauce
1 canned pork roast, weighing 1 pound, 14 ounces
2 cans (about 14 ounces each) fried rice

1 Sauté celery in vegetable oil just until crisply tender in a large frying pan.
2 Stir in water chestnuts, chow mein and sauce, and soy sauce. Heat, stirring lightly, just until bubbly.
3 Scrape gelatin coating from pork roast with a knife, then cut the meat into large cubes. Sprinkle over chow-mein mixture in frying pan; cover. Heat 8 to 10 minutes, or until meat is heated through.
4 Prepare fried rice, following label directions. Serve with chow mein.

Captain's Cake
Bake at 350° for 40 minutes, then broil for 2 minutes. Makes 1 cake, 13x9x2

1 package lemon cake mix
 Eggs
 Water
6 tablespoons (¾ stick) butter or margarine
1 cup firmly packed light brown sugar
1 can (3½ ounces) flaked coconut
1 can (about 4 ounces) toasted sliced almonds
1 can (about 14 ounces) mixed Hawaiian fruits, drained

1 Grease a baking pan, 13x9x2; flour lightly, tapping out any excess.

688

2 Prepare cake mix with eggs and water, following label directions. Pour into prepared pan.
3 Bake in moderate oven (350°) 40 minutes, or until center springs back when lightly pressed with fingertip; remove from oven to a wire rack. Raise temperature to BROIL.
4 While cake bakes, melt butter or margarine in a medium-size saucepan; stir in brown sugar; remove from heat. Stir in coconut and almonds; fold in fruits. Spoon evenly over hot cake.
5 Broil, 4 to 6 inches from heat, 2 minutes, or until topping bubbles. Cool in pan on a wire rack. Cut in squares.

MEALS FOR CAMPERS

CAMPSITE SUPPER
Beef Ball Chili
Spider Biscuit Puffs
Blueberry Bananza
Cherry Cookie Jumbos
Chocolate Milk Shakes
(packaged or canned variety)
Coffee
Toasted Marshmallows

Beef Ball Chili
Makes 6 generous servings

2 pounds ground beef
1 teaspoon salt
2 cans (15 ounces each) chili without beans
1 can (1 pound) stewed tomatoes
1 can (1 pound) red kidney beans
1 can (12 or 16 ounces) whole-kernel corn

1 Season ground beef with salt; shape into 24 meat balls. Sauté slowly, turning several times, until well browned in a heavy kettle or Dutch oven. Spoon off excess drippings.
2 Stir in chili, tomatoes, kidney beans, and corn. Heat slowly, stirring several times, to boiling, then simmer 15 minutes to season and blend flavors.
3 Sprinkle with green-pepper squares, if you wish. Ladle into big bowls; serve with SPIDER BISCUIT PUFFS.

Spider Biscuit Puffs
Makes 6 large puffs

2 cups biscuit mix
½ cup grated Cheddar cheese
¼ teaspoon paprika
⅔ cup milk
1 tablespoon vegetable shortening
¼ cup water

1 Fix your own baker with an 8-inch heavy frying pan and a rack or trivet that will fit into the pan. Grease rack; set over a double-thick strip of foil, 1 inch wide and 12 inches long. (Foil makes a handy lifter for the rack.)

2 Combine biscuit mix, half of the Cheddar cheese, and paprika in a large bowl. Add milk all at once; stir until evenly moist. Drop onto rack in 6 large even mounds.

3 Combine shortening and water in frying pan; heat to boiling; place rack with biscuits in pan. Protecting your hands with potholders, cover pan tightly with a double-thick sheet of foil. Turn heat to medium.

4 Steam biscuits 5 minutes, or until bubbling stops; turn heat to low. Cook 10 minutes; uncover. Sprinkle remaining cheese over biscuits; sprinkle with more paprika, if you wish. Continue cooking 3 minutes longer, or until cheese melts and tops of biscuits are dry. Lift rack from pan by foil handles; remove biscuits from rack with a spatula. Serve hot.

Note to stay-at-home cooks—Prepare dough as above. Bake in oven, following directions on biscuit-mix package for drop biscuits.

Blueberry Bananza
Makes 6 servings

1 can (about 1 pound) vanilla pudding
1 can (about 6 ounces) apricot nectar
2 cups (1 pint) blueberries
6 medium-size bananas

1 Blend pudding and apricot nectar in a bowl or wide-mouth jar.

2 Wash blueberries and stem; peel bananas and slice. Arrange fruits in a large shallow bowl or in individual bowls.

3 Spoon sauce generously over fruit.

Cherry Cookie Jumbos
Bake at 350° for 20 minutes. Makes 1 dozen 4½-inch cookies

1 cup (2 sticks) butter or margarine
1 package (3 or 4 ounces) cream cheese
1 cup sugar
1 egg
1 tablespoon grated orange rind

Rib-sticking camp supper starring Beef Ball Chili.

½ teaspoon almond extract
½ teaspoon salt
2 cups sifted all-purpose flour
2 cups bite-size toasted corn cereal
½ cup finely chopped candied red cherries

1 Cream butter or margarine, cheese, and sugar until fluffy-light in a medium-size bowl. Beat in egg, orange rind, almond extract, and salt.

2 Stir flour, a third at a time, into creamed mixture, blending well to make a soft dough. Fold in cereal.

3 Drop dough, about ⅓ cup for each cookie, 2 inches apart, onto large cookie sheets; sprinkle with cherries and more sugar, if you wish.

4 Bake in moderate oven (350°) 20 minutes, or until lightly golden. Remove carefully from cookie sheets to wire racks with a wide spatula; cool completely.

COOKING ON LOCATION

HOBO'S HEARTY
Cancan Pea Soup
Corned-Beef Pattycakes
Tomatoes in Foil
Ranger Shortcake
Coffee

Cancan Pea Soup
Makes 4 servings

1 can (11¼ ounces) condensed green-pea soup
1 soup can of water
1 can (10½ ounces) condensed chicken-rice soup
1 tablespoon lemon juice

1 Blend pea soup and water until smooth in a medium-size saucepan; stir in chicken soup.
2 Heat slowly, stirring several times, to boiling. Stir in lemon juice; pour into mugs. Serve with unsalted crackers, if you wish.

Corned-Beef Pattycakes
Makes 4 servings, 2 each

1 can (12 ounces) corned beef
Instant mashed potatoes
Water
Salt
Butter or margarine (for potatoes)
1 egg, beaten
2 tablespoons instant minced onion
2 tablespoons butter or margarine (for frying)

1 Shred corned beef with a fork in a medium-size bowl.
2 Prepare 4 cups instant mashed potatoes with water, salt, and butter or margarine, following label directions. (Omit milk called for.) Stir in egg, onion, and corned beef. Divide into 8 even mounds; shape each into a thick patty.
3 Sauté patties in the 2 tablespoons butter or margarine in a large frying pan, turning once, until crusty-brown.

Tomatoes in Foil
Makes 4 servings

4 large firm ripe tomatoes
2 tablespoons butter or margarine
Salt
Pepper
2 tablespoons grated Romano cheese

1 Halve each tomato crosswise. Dot with butter or margarine; sprinkle with salt, pepper, and cheese. Wrap each two halves, side by side, in foil. Place packets on grill.
2 Heat 20 minutes, or until topping melts and tomatoes are hot. Serve in foil wrappers.

Ranger Shortcake
Makes 4 to 6 servings

1 package dessert layers (2 to a package)
3 tablespoons butter or margarine
1 tablespoon sugar
1 can (1 pound, 5 ounces) pineapple pie filling
1 container (4½ ounces) frozen whipped topping, thawed

1 Spread dessert layers with butter or margarine; sprinkle with sugar. Wrap each in foil; place on grill. Heat 3 to 5 minutes.
2 Fold pineapple pie filling into whipped topping in a medium-size bowl.
3 Unwrap dessert layers; spread each generously with pineapple mixture; stack. Cut into wedges.

ANGLER'S REWARD
Skillet Trout
Fisherman's Fried Potatoes
Campfire Beans
Rye Bread
Frosted Ginger Bars
Coffee

Skillet Trout
Makes 4 servings

4 ready-to-cook trout
1 package seasoned coating mix for fish
½ cup vegetable oil

1 Moisten trout; shake with coating mix to cover generously.
2 Sauté in vegetable oil in a large frying pan 4 minutes; turn. Cook 3 to 4 minutes longer, or until fish flakes easily.

Fisherman's Fried Potatoes
Makes 4 servings

1 large onion, coarsely chopped (1 cup)
2 tablespoons bacon drippings
2 cans (1 pound each) white potatoes, drained
   and sliced
1 teaspoon salt
¼ teaspoon pepper

1 Sauté onion in bacon drippings until soft in a frying pan.
2 Stir in potatoes; sprinkle with salt and pepper. Cook, stirring several times, 8 minutes, or until heated through and lightly browned.

Campfire Beans
Makes 4 generous servings

1 can (1 pound) cut green beans, drained
1 can (1 pound) cut wax beans, drained
2 tablespoons butter or margarine
½ teaspoon salt
⅛ teaspoon pepper
2 teaspoons parsley flakes

1 Mound beans in the center of an 18-inch square of double-thick heavy foil. Dot with butter or margarine; sprinkle with salt, pepper, and parsley flakes. Fold foil up around beans and seal tightly. Place on grill over hot coals.
2 Heat 15 to 20 minutes, or until beans are hot.

Frosted Ginger Bars
Bake at 350° for 20 minutes. Makes 16 bars

1 package gingerbread mix
½ cup seedless raisins
1 egg
2 tablespoons vegetable oil
½ cup water
2 teaspoons orange extract
½ cup 10X (confectioners' powdered) sugar

1 Combine gingerbread mix with the raisins in a large bowl; toss lightly with spoon.
2 Beat egg slightly in a small bowl; stir in vegetable oil, water, and orange extract. Pour over gingerbread mixture; beat, following label directions for gingerbread. Spread evenly in a well-greased baking pan, 13x9x2.
3 Bake in moderate oven (350°) 20 minutes, or until firm in center when lightly pressed with fingertip. Cool gingerbread completely in pan on a wire rack.
4 Mix 10X sugar and 1 tablespoon water until smooth in a cup; drizzle, crisscross fashion, on gingerbread. Cut into 16 frosted bars.

MORE MAIN DISHES TO COOK OUT OR CARRY

Picnic Cassoulet
Bake at 400° for 1 hour. Makes 8 generous servings

4 slices bacon, diced
2 pounds boneless lean lamb shoulder, cut in
   1-inch cubes
1 large onion, chopped (1 cup)
¼ pound salami, cut in ¼-inch cubes
2 cans (about 1 pound each) white kidney
   beans
1 can (about 1 pound) stewed tomatoes
1 teaspoon salt
¼ teaspoon pepper
1 bay leaf

1 Sauté bacon until crisp in a large frying pan; remove with a slotted spoon and place in a 10-cup deep baking dish.
2 Brown lamb slowly, about half at a time, in bacon drippings; drain all drippings from pan. Return all meat to pan; cover. Cook slowly 15 minutes. Remove with a slotted spoon and place in baking dish with bacon.
3 Sauté onion until soft in same frying pan; stir in salami and sauté about 2 minutes. Stir in beans and liquid, tomatoes, salt, pepper, and bay leaf; heat to boiling. Stir into meat mixture; cover.
4 Bake in hot oven (400°) 30 minutes; uncover. Bake 30 minutes longer, or until lamb is tender. Remove bay leaf.

Glazed Lamburger Cakes
Makes 6 servings

1½ pounds ground lamb patties
1 egg
½ cup soft bread crumbs (1 slice)
1 small onion, chopped (¼ cup)
5 tablespoons bottled savory sauce
1 teaspoon salt
¼ teaspoon leaf oregano, crumbled
6 slices bacon
2 tablespoons catsup

691

1 Combine lamb, egg, bread crumbs, onion, 1 tablespoon of the savory sauce, salt, and oregano in a medium-size bowl; mix lightly until well blended. Shape into 6 thick patties. Wrap a slice of bacon around each and fasten with a dampened wooden pick.

2 Combine remaining 4 tablespoons savory sauce and catsup in a cup; brush on both sides of patties. Place on grill about 6 inches above hot coals.

3 Grill, turning once and brushing often with remaining catsup mixture, 20 minutes, or until lamb is richly browned and bacon is crisp.

Pocketbook Pork Chops
Makes 8 servings

16 rib pork chops, cut ½ inch thick
 4 teaspoons leaf marjoram, crumbled
 1 large onion, peeled and cut in 8 thin slices
 1 apple, pared, quartered, cored, and sliced thin
 1 can (8 ounces) tomato sauce with mushrooms
 2 tablespoons brown sugar
 1 teaspoon salt
 1 teaspoon ground ginger
 1 cup water
 ¼ cup olive oil or vegetable oil
 ¼ cup cider vinegar

1 Arrange chops on a cutting board in 2 rows of 8 chops each, matching sizes as evenly as possible; sprinkle with marjoram.

2 Cook onion slices in boiling water in a large frying pan 5 minutes; lift out, 1 at a time, with a slotted pancake turner; place on each of 8 chops. Top with apple slices, dividing evenly, then with second pork chop, marjoram side down.

3 Hold each double chop together with dampened wooden picks placed around edges; lace with clean white string and tie. Place chops in a large shallow dish.

4 Mix remaining ingredients in a medium-size bowl; pour over chops; cover. Chill 3 to 4 hours.

5 Remove chops from marinade; place on grill about 6 inches above hot coals. Pour marinade into a saucepan; heat on side of grill.

6 Grill chops, turning and basting often with marinade, 30 to 45 minutes, or until crusty-brown and meat is tender.

Beef Roll Madrid
Makes 6 servings

1½ pounds ground beef
 2 cups soft bread crumbs (4 slices)
 ½ cup evaporated milk
 1 medium-size onion, chopped (½ cup)
 1 cup pitted green olives, chopped
 1 clove of garlic, minced
 2 eggs
 1 teaspoon salt
 ½ teaspoon paprika
 ¼ teaspoon pepper
 ½ cup bottled barbecue sauce

1 Combine all ingredients, except barbecue sauce, in a large bowl; mix lightly until well blended.

2 Shape meat into a 12-inch-long roll on a sheet of heavy foil; wrap tightly and seal lengthwise with a drugstore fold. Fold one end over and over to seal. Stand roll on end; tap gently to settle meat; seal other end.

3 Place roll in its foil cover on grill about 6 inches above hot coals. Grill, turning roll a quarter turn every 10 minutes, 40 minutes.

4 Slide roll far enough from heat to unwrap; open foil and crush it around roll to form a cooking pan. Brush roll generously with barbecue sauce. Continue grilling, turning and brushing often with sauce, until meat is richly browned and as done as you like it.

5 Cut into thick slices; serve as part of a dinner plate, or make into sandwiches with buttered toasted hamburger buns.

El Paso Beef
Bake at 400° for 40 minutes. Makes 6 servings

 1 cup yellow corn meal
 1 cup cold water
 3 cups boiling water
 ½ pound sweet Italian sausages
 ½ pound ground beef
 1 medium-size onion, chopped (½ cup)
 ½ sweet green pepper, chopped (½ cup)
 1 envelope (about 1½ ounces) spaghetti sauce mix
 2 to 3 teaspoons chili powder
 1 can (about 1 pound) tomatoes
 1 can (7 ounces) pitted ripe olives, drained and halved
 1 cup grated Cheddar cheese

1 Stir cornmeal into cold water in a medium-size saucepan; stir in boiling water. Cook slowly, stirring several times, 30 minutes, or until very thick. Pour about half into a shallow 8-cup baking dish, spreading into an even layer. Pour remaining into a greased pan, 9x5x3; chill layer in pan.

2 Peel casings from sausages; break up sausages and brown with ground beef in a large frying pan; push to one side. Stir in onion and green pepper; sauté until soft.

3 Stir in spaghetti sauce mix, chili powder, and tomatoes; heat, stirring constantly, to boiling; remove from heat.

4 Set aside 12 olive halves and ¼ cup of the cheese for toppings in Steps 5 and 6; stir remainder into sauce; pour over corn-meal layer in baking dish.

5 Remove chilled corn-meal layer from pan by turning upside down onto a cutting board; cut into 6 even-size pieces, then halve each diagonally to make 12 wedges. Arrange on top of meat mixture in baking dish; sprinkle with remaining ¼ cup cheese.

6 Bake in hot oven (400°) 40 minutes, or until bubbly. Garnish with remaining olives.

Outfitting the Outdoor Chef

You can't pin cookout weather to the calendar, even in cold climes, because freaky sunny-warm days do pop up. Between May and mid-October, however, there's an abundance of outdoor days, perfect for weekends on a boat, beach or back-country trail. So—be prepared for that spur-of-the-moment urge "to split" that inevitably arrives with each golden sunshiny day.

Outfit the glove compartment of your car with these outdoor necessities and amenities—maps, flashlight, first-aid kit, paper cups, screwdrivers (both standard and Phillips), can opener (multi-purpose), whisk broom, scratch pad and pencil, facial tissues and a sponge (for quick wipe-ups). In the trunk, add to the standard equipment that comes with the car a length of rope, a small shovel, and a blanket. Keep picnic and outdoor cooking equipment at home, ready and raring to go (a handy check-list for alfresco chefs follows).

• • •

CHECKLIST FOR CAMPERS AND ALFRESCO CHEFS:

GLOVE COMPARTMENT
- ☐ Book of road maps or individual maps
- ☐ Small box of paper cups
- ☐ Can opener
- ☐ Box of facial tissues
- ☐ Flashlight (you'll never need new batteries if you use a self-generating model)
- ☐ Small first-aid kit
- ☐ Standard screwdriver
- ☐ Phillips screwdriver
- ☐ Whisk broom
- ☐ Sponge
- ☐ Scratch pad and pencil

UNDER GLOVE COMPARTMENT
- ☐ Auto trash holder

CAR TRUNK
- ☐ Car tools, including jack
- ☐ Spare tire
- ☐ Rope
- ☐ Small shovel
- ☐ Dark-color blanket
- ☐ Umbrella

AT HOME
- ☐ Cold chest (fitted with its own jug or a separate one)
- ☐ 4 cans of "canned ice" (keep these in the freezer when not in use)
- ☐ Plastic food containers
- ☐ Roll of plastic wrap or wax paper
- ☐ Stainless-steel flatware (or disposable plastic or wood flatware)
- ☐ Serving spoons
- ☐ Paper napkins
- ☐ Paper towels
- ☐ Small cutting board
- ☐ Sharp knife
- ☐ Picnic basket or carrying bag to hold flatware, serving spoons, paper supplies, cutting board, knife, and the like
- ☐ Small folding picnic table, or
- ☐ Plastic tablecloth if you go to picnic areas where there are tables
- ☐ Beach towels
- ☐ Towels for swimmers

FOR OUTDOOR COOKING
- ☐ Portable charcoal grill, or
- ☐ LP-gas picnic stove, or
- ☐ Propane-gas stove and broiler
- ☐ Proper fuel
- ☐ Mitts (one for each cook)
- ☐ Barbecue tools
- ☐ Roll of aluminum foil

FOR THE CHILDREN
- ☐ Favorite games that can be played in the car
- ☐ Car seat for the baby
- ☐ Toys

693

COOKING OVER THE COALS

COOKING OVER THE COALS:
COOK TIPS FOR THE OUTDOOR CHEF,
SHOPPING TIPS, THE BARBECUE
WRAP-UP, A COLLECTION OF RECIPES,
GOURMET FEASTS FROM THE GRILL

You can't beat a cookout—for fun, for fellowship or for food, especially if that food is a steak sizzling on the grill, a lordly roast turning on a spit, showy kebabs sputtering over the fire or broiler-fryers turning golden under lavish bastings of barbecue sauce. Charcoal cooking is an American institution, if not invention, and for very good reason. Our meats, fish and fowl are plump and succulent, perfect for cooking over the coals.

On the pages that follow, you'll find dozens of recipes for charcoal-broiling meats on big grills and little, also fire-building and cook tips for the outdoor chef.

● ● ●

COOK TIPS FOR THE OUTDOOR CHEF

Starting Point: The fire
Getting the fire going is the same, whether your grill is a fancy store-bought model or a simple rack propped up on two stones. Unless you live where slow-burning wood is abundant, it's best to buy charcoal briquettes, sold by the bag in varying weights in most supermarkets. They start fast, burn slowly without spitting out sparks, and give an intense heat. Knowing how much charcoal to use is also important; this you'll learn through practice.

For easy starting, buy one of the many packaged starter fuels on the market. Choices are many—liquid, jelly, a combination box of charcoal and lighter, even an electric lighter to plug into an outdoor outlet. Be sure to read label directions, and for complete safety follow them to the letter. Other tips: Keep youngsters away from the grill while you're starting the fire and cooking, and before starting any fire, know how to put it out—fast! Sand is your best helper, so it's smart to keep a small pailful handy.

A single layer of briquettes will take a minimum of 30 minutes to heat through. Briquettes are ready when they turn ash-gray. At night, you can also detect a red glow, but the ash-gray look is your best guide. They hold their heat for a long time, so you needn't be in a rush to start cooking. Budget note: If your fire bed is still active when you finish cooking, pick out

695

Grilled and glistening, a princely, smoky-tender ham.

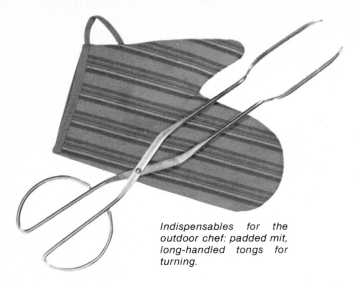

Indispensables for the outdoor chef: padded mit, long-handled tongs for turning.

the briquettes with tongs, dunk them in water, and dry, ready to use another time.

If your food choices seem to be cooking too slowly, it may be that you need a bigger fire bed, or should simply wait awhile before loading the grill. Another possibility is to tap the ash off the briquettes, for it's an insulator. For a fire that appears to be too hot, know-how is simple, too. Lower the fire-box or raise the grill, if they're adjustable. Or move the food to the edge of the grill, away from intense heat.

What about Tools?
You can do nicely with a few carefully chosen ones or go all out—even to a chef's hat. Whatever your choice, do buy good-quality utensils, for they will reward you in long service. A few musts for the new chef:
A long-handle pancake turner for flipping meats, plus a matching spoon for stirring spoonables.
A dipper to use for serving.
A wire broiler basket for grilling and turning several hamburgers at a time.
A two-inch quality paintbrush and heavy saucepan with a flat bottom and heatproof handle for sauce spreader and container.
Sharp knives and a cutting board.
Large easy-grasp salt and pepper shakers.
Asbestos pot holders or mitts.
Roll of heavy foil for all kinds of jobs, from lining the firebox (foil reflects heat faster) to making disposable pans.

Serving Tips for the Chef's Helper
Keep a supply of paper plates, cups, bowls, platters, and napkins on hand, for they make eating out fun and cleanup easy.
Save up a few empty 46-ounce cans (the kind

fruit and vegetable juices come in) and small ones, too, for they make perfect containers for heating barbecue sauces and buttery spreads. They cost nothing and, what's best, are disposable.
Use washcloths for napkins when you entertain, for they stay put in a breeze, wash easily with no ironing, and, if dampened, are ideal for finger-style eating. And your guests will appreciate your thoughtfulness.
Turn oven racks into trays if you need extra-large ones. They're perfect for toting all the paraphernalia that's needed for outdoor cooking.

SHOPPING TIPS FOR THE OUTDOOR CHEF

Your supermarket features the grilling and barbecuing cuts that are most popular and plentiful in your area. But your butcher will be happy to prepare a special cut, too. Whenever possible, order ahead so that he will be able to fill the order during his slack hours. Here are some 20 ways to vary your meat choices for the charcoal grill:
Beef:
Steak: Choose porterhouse, T-bone, club, strip, rib or tenderloin, cut at least 1 inch thick. Grill over hot coals or roast "on the rocks." (Place meat right on the hot gray coals.) Round, rump, chuck and flank steaks are other varieties that take to grilling but should be tenderized first.
Roast: Buy chuck, cut 2 inches thick. Tenderize before grilling.
Short Ribs: Marinate, tenderize or simmer until almost tender before placing on the grill.
Corned-Beef Brisket: Simmer until tender, then brown or glaze on the grill.
Pork:
Chops: For cooking all the way on the grill, buy thin chops (about ½ inch thick), then cook slowly.
Butterfly Chops: They're boneless and an excellent choice for an alfresco feast.
Spareribs: Meaty back ribs rate tops. Simmer first, then glaze over the coals.
Ham Steak: Choose the fully cooked variety, cut from ½ to 1 inch thick.
Canadian Bacon: Cut in ¼-inch-thick slices to serve plain or glazed.
Sausage: Fresh and smoky links are good. Also try Bratwurst, Bockwurst, Mettwurst,

Steak at its very best—cut extra thick and sizzling on an outdoor charcoal grill. To accompany—vegetables grilled in foil.

Knackwurst and Polish sausages for something different.

Lamb:

Chops: Rib, loin or shoulder chops, cut 1 to 1½ inches thick, are best.

Kebabs: Cut meat from the leg or shoulder in 1 to 1½-inch cubes and thread on long skewers.

Riblets: Simmer first, then glaze over the coals.

Patties: Cook ground lamb patties just as you would hamburgers. They make a pleasant change of taste.

Chicken:

Broiler-Fryers: These are the choicest birds for charcoal grilling. Have them halved or quartered, grill plain or glaze.

Parts: Choose legs, thighs or breasts.

Variety Meats:

Liver: Slice calf's or lamb liver thin and grill quickly so that it doesn't toughen and dry. Remember, too, that overcooking destroys the delicacy of liver.

Cold Cuts: Grill thin slices of bologna, ham or salami to make into hot sandwiches or skewer-cook a big chunky roll of bologna to cut into thick slices and eat like steak.

Seafood:

Fish Fillets: Choose your favorite—they're all delicious charcoal-grilled.

Shrimps and Scallops: Thread onto skewers for easy handling on the grill and baste often so that they don't dry out.

THE BARBECUE WRAP-UP

NAME YOUR CHOICE

Foil—Cook in it, freeze in it, bake in it, or store foods in it—that's how versatile this standby is.

Foil is simply a strong, durable, flexible sheet of aluminum, rolled thick or thin. The lightweight kind, popularly known as "regular," comes in 12-inch-wide rolls of 25, 75, or 200 feet.

Broiling or Freezing Foil—or whatever you call it—is heavier, thicker, and stronger to resist splitting and tearing. Most familiar is 18 inches wide, but don't overlook the newer 14-inch width that just fits most broiler pans. Choose this kind for wrapping meats to charcoal-grill, lining casseroles or baking pans, shaping baking containers, or for long freezer storage.

A most-often-asked question: Which side of the foil—shiny or dull—should you place next to the food? Manufacturers tell us it really

doesn't matter, and the reason for the difference is this simple: In rolling aluminum into sheets, the side next to the roller becomes shiny, while the outside has a mat, or dull, finish.

Self-Sealing or Transparent Wraps—Take your pick of plain or textured kinds—both have many uses. Because they cling, they do a superb job of sealing in flavor and aroma and keeping foods fresh. Most cost about a penny for five feet, although introductory offers or specials will often give you an even bigger break on cost. Rolls contain from 50 up to 200 feet and come in varying widths.

Wax Paper—This old-timer, often taken for granted today, is still one of the thriftiest buys when an airtight covering isn't needed. Most brands are triple-waxed, and all come 12 inches wide in varying lengths. Use it to wrap foods for cupboard, refrigerator, or lunch boxes, or to line baking pans or cookie or candy boxes.

Transparent Bags—Look for clear or quilted, in handy boxes or tear-off rolls, all with twist fasteners. Reusable, they come small enough to fit a sandwich or big enough to hold a turkey. Size for size, all cost about the same. To be most economical, keep several sizes on hand.

CUES FOR COOKOUTS

Here are a few reminders on how to use food wraps to simplify outdoor cooking and toting:

Silver Lining: Cover the firebox of your grill with heavy foil before adding briquettes. Come cleanup time, lift out the foil; put the grill away.

Hot Breads: These favorites needn't be taboo outdoors. Just wrap hamburger or frankfurter rolls or a loaf of French bread in heavy foil and place on the side of the grill to heat while your meat cooks.

Custom Cover: No lid for a skillet, kettle, or flat pan that you want to use on the grill? Just cut a piece of foil and fit it tightly over the top of the container.

Dishwasher's Dream: Shape your own throwaway pans from heavy foil for heating potatoes or vegetables on top of the grill. Turn up edges 1½ to 2 inches for sides; pinch corners so pan won't leak. Same idea makes a good juice catcher when you're barbecuing on a spit. Still another help: Bundle single servings of meats or fish in foil, and after cooking, fold foil back and use it as the serving dish.

Cover Up: If you don't have a roasting pan or dish large enough for marinating a roast or turkey, use a jumbo transparent bag. Place the meat and sauce in the bag, seal tightly, and chill. Just remember to turn the bag several times so the meat seasons evenly.

An all-American summer team: thick, juicy hamburgers and golden sweet corn-on-the-cob fairly dripping with butter!

AN OUTDOOR TIMETABLE FOR GRILLING STEAK, AT ROOM TEMPERATURE

Tender Cuts

Cut	Approximate weight	Approximate thickness	Approximate minutes per side			Servings
			Rare	Medium	Well done	
T-bone	2½ to 3 pounds	1 inch	5 minutes	6 minutes	8 minutes	3
Porterhouse	3 to 3½ pounds	2 inches	10 minutes	14 minutes	16 minutes	4
	3½ to 5 pounds	3 inches	16 minutes	20 minutes	30 minutes	6
Sirloin	3¼ pounds	1½ inches	12 minutes	14 minutes	16 minutes	6
	4½ pounds	2 inches	20 minutes	22 minutes	24 minutes	4 to 5
Strip Steak	¾ pound	1 inch	5 minutes	7 minutes	8 minutes	1 to 2
Rib Steak	12 to 14 ounces	1 inch	5 minutes	6 minutes	8 minutes	1
Filet	4 to 6 ounces	1 inch	4 minutes	6 minutes	—	1

Less Tender Cuts Marinated or Tenderized*

Cut	Approximate weight	Approximate thickness	Approximate minutes per side	Servings
			Rare	
Round Steak	3 to 3½ pounds	2 inches	17 minutes	4 to 6
Skirt Steak	¾ pound	—	5 minutes	2
Flank Steak	1½ pounds	—	5 minutes	4
Chuck Steak	1½ pounds	1 inch	12 minutes	4
	2 to 4 pounds	1½ inches	17 minutes	6 to 8
Sirloin tip, sliced	¾ pound	1 inch	17 minutes	1 to 2

*For using instant meat tenderizer, see label directions

A great French favorite—Steak au Poivre—takes to the great outdoors! It's charcoal grilled.

700

Grilled Steak au Poivre

The success of this popular steak depends on cracked pepper; ground pepper will ruin the dish. To crack your pepper, put the peppercorns into a paper or plastic bag and crush them with a rolling pin or meat mallet. Or buy cracked pepper in any supermarket. As for quantities, experience will tell you after you have tried the recipe; you might like less pepper or you might like more.
Makes 6 to 8 servings

1 sirloin steak, about 2 inches thick, weighing about 4 pounds
2 tablespoons cracked pepper
Salt

1 Wipe steak with damp paper toweling. Using your fingers and heel of hand press half of the pepper into each side of the steak. Let stand at room temperature for 1 hour.
2 Grill about 5 inches from hot coals, about 8 to 10 minutes on each side for medium rare. Sprinkle with salt when removed from heat.
Note—For a showy touch, flame the steak. Transfer the steak to a hot platter. Warm ¼ cup brandy; pour over steak; ignite.

Piquant Flank Steak

When you baste meats on the grill, use, instead of a brush, a bunch of fresh herbs (washed, of course, and tied), such as parsley, rosemary,

tarragon, thyme and so on, either singly or in combinations. They add enormously to the meat's flavor. Just dip the bunch of herbs into the marinade or basting sauce and slosh it on the meat. Flank steak, as all economical cuts, should be carved on the diagonal, into thin slices, for the best eating.
Makes 4 to 6 servings

1 cup tomato juice
¼ cup minced onion or green onion
¼ cup minced green pepper
¼ cup minced celery
¼ cup olive oil
1 tablespoon vinegar
1 to 2 garlic cloves, minced
1 tablespoon chili powder
¼ teaspoon salt
1 flank steak, weighing about 2 pounds
    Unseasoned meat tenderizer

1 Combine tomato juice, onion, green pepper, celery, olive oil, vinegar, garlic, chili powder and salt in a small saucepan. Bring to boiling; reduce heat; cover. Simmer 15 minutes; cool.
2 Trim steak of any excess fat and membrane. Sprinkle meat tenderizer on steak, following label directions. Place in a shallow glass baking dish and pour cooled marinade over the meat. Refrigerate for 1 hour. Remove from marinade; reserve the marinade.
3 Grill about 4 inches from hot coals, 3 to 4 minutes on each side for rare. Baste with reserved marinade.
4 Carve on the diagonal in thin slices.

Steak Sauces and Butters
Serving different sauces or butters with steaks glorifies the more economical cuts as well as hamburger.

Salsa Fria
The most popular of Western sauces and an old California custom at barbecues, taken from the Spanish. Literally, the words mean "cold sauce" but, in practice, they refer to any uncooked tomato sauce.

2 pounds very ripe tomatoes
1 cup finely chopped onion
1 to 4 canned green chilis (from a 4-ounce can), chopped fine (amount depends on degree of hotness desired)
2 tablespoons vegetable oil
1 teaspoon salt
¼ teaspoon freshly ground pepper
    Chopped fresh coriander to taste*
    OR: 1 teaspoon ground oregano
1 to 2 tablespoons cider vinegar (optional)

1 Dip tomatoes in boiling water for 15 seconds; slip off skins.
2 Chop tomatoes; combine with onion, chili, oil, salt, pepper, coriander or oregano and vinegar in a large bowl. Cover; season in the refrigerator for at least 2 hours. Serve chilled, with meats.
*Fresh coriander resembles parsley but has a distinctive flavor of its own.

Maître d'Hôtel Butter
Makes about ⅔ cup

½ cup (1 stick) butter or margarine, softened
2 tablespoons finely minced parsley
2 tablespoons finely minced chives
2 tablespoons lemon juice

1 Blend butter or margarine, parsley and chives in a small bowl. Add lemon juice, a little at a time.
2 Turn out onto wax paper; shape into a 1½-inch roll. Wrap tightly and refrigerate until firm. Cut into slices and serve 1 slice on each serving of meat.

Blue Cheese or Roquefort Butter
Makes about ¾ cup

½ cup blue or Roquefort cheese
4 tablespoons (½ stick) butter or margarine, softened
2 tablespoons sherry, white wine, brandy or cream

1 Remove cheese and butter or margarine from refrigerator. Crumble the cheese. Allow both to stand at room temperature about 2 hours, or until soft.
2 Mash cheese with the butter in a small bowl. Use a fork first and then a spoon. Stir in sherry and mix to a smooth paste. Turn into a bowl and spoon over meats. (This may be prepared ahead and refrigerated, covered; bring back to room temperature.)

Diable Steak-Roast
Double topper of mustard and golden crumbs turns thick sirloin into inviting fare.
Makes 8 servings

701

1 *sirloin steak, cut 2 inches thick (about 4 pounds)*
¼ *cup prepared mustard*
2 *large sweet green peppers, trimmed, seeded, and sliced into rings*
2 *large sweet red peppers, trimmed, seeded, and sliced into rings*
2 *tablespoons butter or margarine*
2 *tablespoons vegetable oil*
   CRUMB TOPPING *(recipe follows)*

1 Remove steak from refrigerator 1 hour before cooking. Trim off any excess fat, then score remaining fat edge every inch so that meat will lie flat on grill.
2 Spread steak with mustard; let stand at room temperature to season.
3 When ready to cook meat, rub hot grill with a few fat trimmings to help prevent sticking. Place steak on grill about 6 inches above hot coals.
4 Grill 10 minutes; turn. Grill 10 minutes longer for rare, or until steak is done as you like it. Remove from grill.
5 While meat cooks, sauté green- and red-pepper rings in butter or margarine until soft in a large frying pan at edge of grill; keep hot.
6 Brush steak all over with vegetable oil; pat CRUMB TOPPING over top of meat; return to grill and heat just until crumbs are set.
7 Remove steak to a cutting board or large platter; place pepper rings around edge. Slice steak ¼ inch thick.

   CRUMB TOPPING—Place 6 slices white bread on a cookie sheet; toast in slow oven (300°) 30 minutes, or until dry, crisp, and richly golden; cool. Crush with a rolling pin. Melt 4 tablespoons (½ stick) butter or margarine in a medium-size saucepan; add bread crumbs; toss to mix well. Makes about 3 cups.

702

All-American Steak Broil
Too popular to be forgotten—that's steak with sautéed onions and mushrooms.
Makes 8 servings

1 *sirloin steak, cut 1½ inches thick (about 4 pounds)*
⅔ *cup olive oil or vegetable oil*
⅓ *cup wine vinegar or cider vinegar*
½ *teaspoon salt*
½ *teaspoon sugar*
½ *teaspoon leaf thyme, crumbled*
¼ *teaspoon pepper*

2 *large onions, peeled, sliced, and separated into rings*
3 *tablespoons butter or margarine*
1 *can (6 ounces) whole mushrooms, drained*

1 Remove steak from refrigerator 1 hour before cooking. Trim off any excess fat, then score remaining fat edge every inch so that meat will lie flat on grill. Place steak in a shallow pan.
2 Mix olive oil or vegetable oil, wine vinegar or cider vinegar, salt, sugar, thyme, and pepper in a small bowl; pour over steak; cover. Let stand at room temperature to season.
3 When ready to cook meat, rub hot grill with a few fat trimmings to help prevent sticking. Remove steak from marinade and place on grill about 6 inches above hot coals.
4 Grill, brushing several times with marinade from pan, 10 minutes; turn. Grill 10 minutes longer for rare, or until steak is done as you like it.
5 While meat cooks, sauté onion rings in butter or margarine until soft in a large frying pan at edge of grill; stir in mushrooms; keep hot.
6 Remove steak to a cutting board or large platter; spoon onions and mushrooms around edge. Slice steak ¼ inch thick.

●

Sicilian Beef
Grill seasoned round steak, then slice and serve with a pungent tomato-garlic sauce.
Makes 6 servings

1 *round steak, cut 1 inch thick (about 2½ pounds)*
1 *envelope instant meat marinade*
⅔ *cup tomato juice*
3 *medium-size onions, chopped (1½ cups)*
1 *clove garlic, minced*
3 *tablespoons vegetable oil*
4 *medium-size tomatoes, peeled and chopped*
1 *teaspoon salt*
1 *teaspoon leaf marjoram, crumbled*
¼ *teaspoon seasoned pepper*

1 Remove steak from refrigerator 15 minutes before cooking. Trim off any excess fat, then score remaining fat edge every inch so that meat will lie flat on grill. Place steak in a shallow pan.
2 Mix meat marinade and tomato juice in a 1-cup measure; pour over steak; pierce steak all over with a fork. Let stand at room temperature to season.
3 When ready to cook meat, rub hot grill with a few fat trimmings to help prevent sticking. Remove steak from marinade and place on grill

What every hungry steak lover dreams of: a super-thick, rare hunk of sirloin. This one is crumb crusted.

about 6 inches above hot coals. (Set marinade aside for sauce in Step 5.)

4 Grill 6 minutes; turn. Grill 6 minutes longer for rare, or until steak is done as you like it.

5 While meat cooks, sauté onions and garlic until soft in vegetable oil in a large frying pan at edge of grill; stir in tomatoes, salt, marjoram, and pepper. Simmer 10 minutes; stir in marinade.

6 Remove steak to a cutting board or large platter; carve into ¼-inch-thick slices; arrange slices in sauce. Serve from frying pan.

●

Barbecued Beef Medallions
Each goes in and out of the frying pan in less than 5 minutes, so they're a good choice for a crowd.
Makes 4 servings

COOKING OVER THE COALS

8 individual boneless steaks (round or chuck),
   each cut ¼ inch thick
   Instant unseasoned meat tenderizer
1 clove garlic, peeled
2 tablespoons olive oil or vegetable oil
1 cup bottled barbecue sauce
½ cup grated mozzarella or pizza cheese

1 Moisten steaks and sprinkle with tenderizer, following label directions.
2 Rub the inside of a large frying pan with garlic clove; add olive oil or vegetable oil. Set pan on grill about 4 inches above hot coals; heat just until oil is hot. Place steaks in pan.
3 Sauté, turning once, 2 minutes; add barbecue sauce. Cook 1 minute longer; sprinkle with grated cheese. Heat just until cheese starts to melt. Serve as is, or on toasted split rolls.

Sombrero Steak

Like a spicy-hot flavor? This meat has it with both chili powder and a generous measure of red pepper seasoning.
Makes 6 servings

1 round steak, cut 1 inch thick (about 2½ pounds)
1 cup vegetable oil
½ cup cider vinegar
2 teaspoons chili powder
1 teaspoon leaf oregano, crumbled
¼ teaspoon garlic powder
¼ teaspoon liquid red pepper seasoning
   Instant unseasoned meat tenderizer

1 Remove steak from refrigerator 1 hour before cooking. Trim off any excess fat, then score remaining fat edge every inch so that meat will lie flat on grill. Place steak in a shallow pan.
2 Mix vegetable oil, vinegar, chili powder, oregano, garlic powder, and liquid red pepper seasoning in a small bowl; pour over steak. Let stand at room temperature to season.
3 When ready to cook meat, rub hot grill with a few fat trimmings to help prevent sticking.
4 Remove steak from marinade; sprinkle with tenderizer, following label directions. Place on grill about 6 inches above hot coals; brush with part of the marinade.
5 Grill 6 minutes; turn. Grill, brushing with remaining marinade, 6 minutes longer for rare, or until steak is done as you like it.
6 Remove to a cutting board or large platter; carve into ¼-inch-thick slices.

London Broil

Grill flank steak the way you like it best, slice, and dunk into your choice of peppy sauces.
Makes 6 servings

1 flank steak, weighing about 2 pounds
   Instant unseasoned meat tenderizer
   Vegetable oil
   SOY DIP (recipe follows)
   HORSERADISH ZIP (recipe follows)

1 Moisten steak and sprinkle with tenderizer, following label directions.
2 When ready to cook meat, brush hot grill with vegetable oil to help prevent sticking. Place steak on grill about 4 inches above hot coals.
3 Grill 5 minutes; turn. Grill 5 minutes longer for rare, or until steak is done as you like it.
4 Remove steak to a cutting board or large platter; carve diagonally into ¼-inch-thick slices. Serve with SOY DIP and HORSERADISH ZIP.
  SOY DIP—Blend ½ cup soy sauce, ¼ cup wine vinegar or cider vinegar, 1 teaspoon garlic powder, and ½ teaspoon ground ginger in a small bowl. Chill at least an hour to blend flavors. Makes about ¾ cup.
  HORSERADISH ZIP—Blend ½ cup bottled chili sauce, 2 tablespoons prepared horseradish, 1 tablespoon lemon juice, and 1 teaspoon Worcestershire sauce in a small bowl. Chill at least an hour to blend flavors. Makes about ¾ cup.

Stuffed Steakettes

Cut a pocket in small steaks labeled MINUTE or CHICKEN, fill with herb butter, and grill quickly.
Makes 6 servings

6 individual boneless beefsteaks (round or chuck), eacn cut ½ inch thick
   Instant unseasoned meat tenderizer
6 tablespoons (¾ stick) butter or margarine
¼ cup chopped parsley
2 tablespoons finely cut chives
½ teaspoon dry mustard
2 tablespoons bottled gravy coloring
   Vegetable oil

1 Cut a slit about 3 inches wide and 2 inches deep in one side of each steak to form a pocket for stuffing. Moisten steaks and sprinkle with tenderizer, following label directions.
2 Blend butter or margarine, parsley, chives, and mustard in a small bowl; spread inside pockets in steaks, dividing evenly. Brush outside of each with gravy coloring.

3 When ready to cook meat, brush hot grill with vegetable oil to help prevent sticking. Place steaks on grill about 4 inches above hot coals.
4 Grill 3 minutes; turn. Grill 3 minutes longer for rare, or until steaks are done as you like them. Serve as is, or on toasted split rolls.

Beefeaters' Bargain
"Rosemary for remembrance" adds the subtle tang to chuck steak.
Makes 8 servings

1 blade-bone chuck beefsteak, cut 2 inches thick (about 4 pounds)
¼ cup vegetable oil
2 tablespoons leaf rosemary, finely crumbled
Instant unseasoned meat tenderizer
2 tablespoons butter or margarine

1 Remove steak from refrigerator 1 hour before cooking. Trim off any excess fat, then score remaining fat edge every inch so that meat will lie flat on grill.
2 Brush steak all over with vegetable oil; pat rosemary onto both sides. Let stand at room temperature to season.
3 When ready to cook meat, rub hot grill with a few fat trimmings to help prevent sticking. Moisten steak and sprinkle with tenderizer, following label directions. Place on grill about 6 inches above hot coals.
4 Grill 10 minutes; turn. Grill 10 minutes longer for rare, or until steak is done as you like it.
5 Remove to a cutting board or large platter; dot with butter or margarine; let melt into steak. Slice steak ¼ inch thick.

Gridiron Steak
Curry, sherry, soy, and ginger season the meat before and during grilling for a delightfully appealing flavor.
Makes 6 servings

1 round-bone chuck beefsteak, cut 2 inches thick (about 3 pounds)
1 medium-size onion, chopped (1 cup)
¼ cup vegetable oil
1 tablespoon curry powder
½ cup dry sherry
¼ cup soy sauce
½ teaspoon ground ginger
Instant unseasoned meat tenderizer

1 Remove steak from refrigerator 1 hour before cooking. Trim off any excess fat, then score remaining fat edge every inch so that meat will lie flat on grill. Place steak in a shallow pan.

2 Sauté onion in vegetable oil until soft in a medium-size frying pan; stir in curry powder; cook 1 minute; remove from heat. Stir in sherry, soy sauce, and ginger; pour over steak; cover. Let stand at room temperature, turning several times, to season.
3 When ready to cook meat, rub hot grill with a few fat trimmings to help prevent sticking. Remove steak from marinade; sprinkle with tenderizer, following label directions. Place on grill about 6 inches above hot coals.
4 Grill, brushing several times with marinade from pan, 10 minutes; turn. Grill 10 minutes longer for rare, or until steak is done as you like it.
5 Remove to a cutting board or large platter. Slice ¼ inch thick.

Over-the-Coals Steak Roll
Twirl flank steak around a mellow bacon-and-egg-stuffing, then cook crusty-brown on the grill. Makes 6 servings

1 flank steak, weighing about 2 pounds
4 slices bacon, cut in 1-inch pieces
1 medium-size onion, chopped (½ cup)
4 slices white bread, cubed
3 hard-cooked eggs, shelled and chopped
½ cup chopped stuffed green olives
½ cup vegetable oil
1 teaspoon seasoned salt
¼ teaspoon seasoned pepper
2 tablespoons bottled steak sauce

1 Ask your meatman to split flank steak, butterfly fashion. Or, you can do it yourself with a sharp long-blade knife. Work slowly, cutting with a sawing motion as evenly as possible. Pound steak slightly with a mallet or rolling pin to make evenly thin.
2 Sauté bacon until crisp in a large frying pan; remove with a slotted spoon and drain on paper toweling. Stir onion into drippings in same pan; sauté until soft; remove from heat. Stir in bread cubes, eggs, olives, and bacon; toss lightly until evenly moist.
3 Lay steak flat on counter top; brush with about 1 tablespoon of the vegetable oil; spread stuffing over steak to within 1 inch of edges.
4 Starting at a long side of steak, roll up tightly, tucking in any loose stuffing; tie every 2 inches with strong white string.
5 Brush hot grill with vegetable oil to help prevent sticking. Place steak roll on grill about 10 inches above hot coals.

705

Grills are wonderfully accommodating! They will broil burgers and heat the pot of coffee all at the same time.

6 Mix remaining vegetable oil with seasoned salt and pepper in a small saucepan; brush part over steak roll.

7 Grill, turning and brushing with oil mixture every 10 minutes, 1 hour.

8 Stir steak sauce into remaining oil mixture; brush part over roll. Continue grilling, brushing several times with remaining oil mixture, 10 minutes, or until meat is tender and richly browned.

9 Remove roll to a cutting board or large platter; snip off strings. Carve roll into 1-inch-thick slices.

Pepper Lamb Steaks

An outdoor luxury! Flavor is spicy-hot so you may want to start with less pepper to suit your taste.
Makes 4 servings

4 lamb steaks, cut ½ inch thick
  Instant unseasoned meat tenderizer
  Seasoned salt
1 tablespoon peppercorns

1 Moisten steaks and sprinkle with meat tenderizer, following label directions; sprinkle lightly with seasoned salt.

2 Crush peppercorns with a rolling pin. (Job is easy if you place the peppercorns in a transparent bag.) Press onto each side of steaks. Place steaks on grill about 6 inches above hot coals.

3 Grill, turning once, 12 minutes for medium, or until meat is done as you like it.

Fruit-Glazed Pork Chops

Simmer chops until almost tender indoors, then glaze sparkly golden on the grill.
Makes 6 servings

6 loin pork chops, cut 1 inch thick
½ cup apricot marmalade
⅓ cup bottled smoke-flavor barbecue sauce
¼ cup light corn syrup
1 teaspoon prepared mustard
½ teaspoon ground cloves

1 Simmer pork chops, covered, in boiling salted water in a medium-size saucepan 20 minutes, or until almost tender; drain.

2 Press apricot marmalade through a sieve into a small saucepan; stir in barbecue sauce, corn syrup, mustard, and cloves; brush part over one side of chops. Place chops, sauce side down, on grill about 6 inches above hot coals; brush other side with sauce.

3 Grill, turning and brushing several times with remaining apricot sauce, 20 minutes, or until chops are tender and richly glazed.

Grilled Hamburger Squares

Makes 8 servings

2 pounds ground beef
2 eggs
1 medium-size onion, chopped (½ cup)
1 cup grated Cheddar cheese (4 ounces)

2 *teaspoons salt*
½ *teaspoon celery salt*
¼ *teaspoon pepper*
16 *slices bread*

1 Mix ground beef lightly with eggs, onion, cheese, and seasonings until well blended; divide into 8 portions.
2 Press each into a square the same size as bread slice on a square of wax paper or foil.
3 Grill squares over hot coals until meat is done as you like it.
4 Toast bread on grill, then butter, if you wish. Put together, sandwich style, with meat squares. Serve plain or with catsup, prepared horseradish-mustard, or canned French fried onion rings.

Mulholland Burgers
Makes 8 servings

2 *pounds ground beef*
1 *envelope instant meat marinade*
⅔ *cup water*
8 *large poppy-seed rolls, split and toasted*

1 Shape ground beef into 8 patties about ¾ inch thick; place in a shallow dish; chill.
2 Just before cooking, mix meat marinade and water, following label directions; pour over patties; turn to coat all over.
3 Grill over hot coals, brushing several times with remaining marinade in dish, until meat is done as you like it.
4 Put together, sandwich style, with toasted rolls. Serve with sweet pickles and potato or corn chips, if you wish.

Burgers Milanese
Makes 8 servings

2 *pounds ground beef*
½ *cup bottled Italian salad dressing*
1 *package (8 ounces) sliced mozzarella or pizza cheese, cut in triangles*
16 *slices Italian bread, toasted*

1 Shape ground beef into 8 patties about ¾ inch thick; place in a shallow dish. Pour salad dressing over; turn patties to coat well with dressing; chill, turning several times, about 15 minutes to season.
2 When ready to cook, remove patties from dressing. Grill over hot coals, brushing several

times with remaining dressing in dish, until meat is almost as done as you like it.
3 Top each patty with 2 or 3 cheese triangles; continue grilling 1 to 2 minutes longer, or just until cheese melts slightly.
4 Put each patty together, sandwich style, with toasted bread slices.

Smoky Beef Burgers
Makes 8 servings

2 *pounds ground beef*
1 *medium-size onion, grated*
2 *teaspoons salt*
½ *teaspoon leaf oregano, crumbled*
¼ *teaspoon pepper*
½ *cup bottled smoke-flavor barbecue sauce*
3 *tablespoons water*
8 *English muffins, split and toasted*

1 Mix ground beef lightly with onion, salt, oregano, pepper, and 2 tablespoons of the barbecue sauce; shape into 8 patties about ¾ inch thick. Mix remaining barbecue sauce and water.
2 Grill patties over hot coals, brushing several times with barbecue-sauce mixture, until meat is done as you like it.
3 Put together, sandwich style, with toasted muffins.

Yorkville Special
Makes 6 servings

2 *pounds ground beef*
2 *teaspoons salt*
½ *teaspoon caraway seeds*
2 *cups coleslaw (from a 1-pound container)*
6 *slices rye bread, buttered*
  Paprika

1 Mix ground beef lightly with salt and caraway seeds; shape into 6 patties about 1 inch thick.
2 Grill patties over hot coals until meat is done as you like it.
3 Drain coleslaw well; spoon onto each slice of bread to form a rest; top with a meat patty; sprinkle with paprika.

Pepper Burgers
Makes 6 servings

1 *envelope instant beef broth*
  OR: 1 teaspoon granulated beef bouillon
¼ *cup boiling water*
2 *pounds ground beef*
1 *tablespoon Worcestershire sauce*
2 *teaspoons soy sauce*

707

¼ teaspoon salt
½ teaspoon freshly ground black pepper
6 split hamburger buns
1 can (about 3 ounces) French fried onion rings

1 Dissolve beef broth in boiling water in a 1-cup measure.
2 Combine with ground beef, Worcestershire sauce, soy sauce, and salt in a medium-size bowl; mix lightly until well blended. Shape into 6 big patties. Sprinkle each side of patties generously with pepper, pressing it into meat lightly with hands. Place on grill about 6 inches above hot coals.
3 Grill, turning once, 10 to 20 minutes, or until meat is as done as you like it.
4 Toast buns alongside patties on grill, then butter, if you wish. Place meat patties in buns; top each patty with onion rings.

A Few Simple Tricks with Grilled Burgers
Grill burgers good and brown before turning. And flip only once.

Prevent sticking by brushing grill or patties with a little vegetable oil; or for meat, use vegetable oil mixed with a seasoner of your choice.

Shape hamburger patties around a small piece of cracked ice. As the meat grills, the ice will melt and give the burger a special juiciness. Or moisten both sides of the patty with a few drops of cold water.

Make one giant 1-inch-thick patty instead of several individual burgers and, as it grills, brush with barbecue or Worcestershire sauce for a deep rich color. Simply cut into wedges for serving.

708

ZIPPY SAUCES TO BRUSH ON STEAKS OR BURGERS AS THEY GRILL

Basic Barbecue Sauce
Makes 3 cups

1 cup light molasses
1 cup prepared mustard
1 cup cider vinegar

Combine all ingredients in a 4-cup jar with tight-fitting lid; shake well to mix. Store in refrigerator.

Variations:
GINGER-RICH SAUCE—Mix 1 cup BASIC BARBECUE SAUCE with ½ cup ginger marmalade and 1 teaspoon ground ginger. Makes 1½ cups.
ZING SAUCE—Mix 1 cup BASIC BARBECUE SAUCE with ¼ cup catsup, ¼ cup vegetable oil, and 2 tablespoons Worcestershire sauce. Makes 1½ cups.
ITALIAN HERB SAUCE—Mix 1 cup BASIC BARBECUE SAUCE with ½ cup chili sauce and ½ teaspoon oregano. Makes 1½ cups.
PEPPY TOMATO SAUCE—Mix 1 cup BASIC BARBECUE SAUCE with ½ cup tomato juice and ½ teaspoon cracked or freshly ground pepper. Makes 1½ cups.

Diable Sauce
Makes about 2 cups

¾ cup prepared mustard
½ cup molasses
½ cup cider vinegar
1 tablespoon Worcestershire sauce
¼ teaspoon liquid red pepper seasoning

1 Combine all ingredients in a small bowl; beat until well blended.
2 Spread sparingly on hamburgers, for this sauce is **hot.**
3 Store any left over in a tightly covered jar in the refrigerator.

Red Soy Sauce
Makes 2½ cups

2 cans (8 ounces each) tomato sauce
1 medium-size onion, chopped (½ cup)
1 clove garlic, minced
¼ cup soy sauce
2 tablespoons sugar
1 teaspoon dry mustard
⅛ teaspoon cayenne

1 Combine all ingredients in a medium-size bowl; stir until well blended.
2 Store any left over in a tightly covered jar in the refrigerator.

GOURMET SAUCES TO TOP COOKED STEAKS OR BURGERS

Javanese Peanut Sauce
Makes 1¼ cups

1 small onion, finely chopped (¼ cup)
2 tablespoons peanut oil or vegetable oil
¼ teaspoon ground cardamom
½ cup cream-style peanut butter
¼ cup firmly packed brown sugar
¼ cup soy sauce
¼ cup lemon juice
¼ teaspoon liquid red pepper seasoning

1 Sauté onion in peanut oil or vegetable oil just until soft in a small frying pan; stir in cardamom. Let stand to cool slightly.
2 Blend peanut butter with brown sugar in a small bowl; stir in remaining ingredients, then cooled onion mixture.
3 Let stand at room temperature until serving time.

Horseradish-Almond Sauce
Makes about 1¼ cups

¼ cup toasted slivered almonds (from a 5-ounce can)
2 teaspoons butter or margarine
2 teaspoons all-purpose flour
1 teaspoon sugar
¼ teaspoon salt
1 small can evaporated milk (⅔ cup)
⅓ cup milk
2 tablespoons prepared horseradish

1 Sauté almonds in butter or margarine until golden-brown in a small saucepan; remove from heat.
2 Stir in flour, sugar, and salt; cook, stirring constantly, just until bubbly. Stir in evaporated milk and milk; continue cooking and stirring until sauce thickens and boils 1 minute.
3 Stir in horseradish; serve warm.

Mock Bearnaise Sauce
Makes about 1 cup

½ cup apple juice
1 tablespoon tarragon vinegar
1 tablespoon finely chopped onion or shallots
⅛ teaspoon freshly ground pepper
1 sprig parsley
½ teaspoon dried tarragon leaves
2 egg yolks
½ cup (1 stick) butter or margarine, melted
    Dash of cayenne
1 teaspoon chopped parsley

1 Combine apple juice, vinegar, onion or shallots, pepper, parsley sprig, and tarragon in a small saucepan. Heat to boiling, then simmer, uncovered, 8 to 10 minutes, or until liquid measures about ⅓ cup; strain into a cup.
2 Beat egg yolks slightly in the top of a double boiler; stir in about ⅓ of the melted butter or margarine. Place top over simmering, *not boiling,* water.
3 Beat in strained liquid, alternately with remaining melted butter or margarine; continue beating, keeping top over simmering water, until mixture is fluffy-thick. Remove from heat at once.
4 Stir in cayenne and chopped parsley. Serve warm.

FANCY RELISHES TO SERVE WITH PLAIN STEAKS OR BURGERS

Ripe-Olive Chop-Chop
Makes about 5 cups

3 cans (2¼ ounces each) chopped ripe olives
1½ cups finely chopped celery
1 cup finely chopped dill pickle (about 4 medium-size)
½ cup finely chopped onion
1 clove garlic, minced
1 can (2 ounces) anchovy fillets
½ cup vegetable oil
¼ cup wine vinegar or cider vinegar
¼ teaspoon pepper

1 Combine olives, celery, dill pickle, onion, and garlic; toss lightly to mix.
2 Drain oil from anchovies into olive mixture; cut anchovies into tiny pieces and stir in with vegetable oil, vinegar, and pepper; toss well to mix; cover. Chill several hours or overnight.

709

Corn Piquant
Makes about 4 cups

1 teaspoon sugar
½ teaspoon salt
¼ teaspoon paprika
¾ cup vegetable oil
¼ cup cider vinegar
1 tablespoon prepared horseradish
1½ teaspoons Worcestershire sauce
2 drops liquid red pepper seasoning
2 cans (12 or 16 ounces each) whole-kernel corn, drained

1 Combine all ingredients, except corn, in a jar with tight-fitting lid; shake well to mix.
2 Pour over corn; toss lightly to mix; cover. Chill several hours or overnight.

Spareribs Kun Koki

Zippy lime adds the most refreshingly different flavor to these popular outdoor-cooked favorites.
Makes 4 servings

4 pounds fresh spareribs
½ cup catsup
¼ cup lime juice
¼ cup soy sauce
¼ cup honey

1 Place spareribs on grill about 12 inches from hot coals. Grill, turning several times, 1 hour, or until meat is almost tender.
2 Mix catsup, lime juice, and soy sauce in a small saucepan; brush part over ribs. Continue grilling, turning and brushing several times with sauce mixture, 20 minutes.
3 Blend honey into remaining sauce; brush over ribs. Grill, turning and brushing once or twice with remaining honey mixture, 10 minutes, or until meat is tender and richly glazed.
4 Remove ribs to a carving board; cut into serving-size pieces of 1 or 2 ribs each. Serve with onion halves cooked in foil, if you wish. (To fix them, halve large onions; sprinkle with salt and pepper; wrap in foil. Cook on grill beside ribs 45 minutes, or until tender. Open foil packets; sprinkle onions lightly with paprika.)

Curried Spareribs

Enjoy them, finger style, right down to the bone. Mellow curry glaze adds the inviting flavor.
Makes 4 servings

4 pounds fresh spareribs
6 tablespoons instant minced onion
½ teaspoon peppercorns
Water
1 tablespoon curry powder
2 tablespoons butter or margarine
2 teaspoons salt
1 jar (about 5 ounces) baby-pack applesauce
2 tablespoons lemon juice

1 Cut spareribs into serving-size pieces of 2 or 3 ribs each; combine with 4 tablespoons of the

onion and peppercorns in a kettle. Add water to cover; cover. Simmer 45 minutes; remove ribs from liquid.
2 While ribs simmer, cook curry powder slowly in butter or margarine in a small saucepan 2 minutes; stir in remaining 2 tablespoons onion, salt, applesauce, lemon juice, and 2 tablespoons water.
3 Place ribs in a single layer on grill about 10 inches from hot coals; brush with part of the curry sauce. Grill, turning and brushing often with remaining curry sauce, 45 minutes, or until meat is tender and richly browned.

Hobo Ribs

Best-ever finger food—crispy outside and sweet and smoky next to the bone.
Makes 4 servings

4 pounds fresh spareribs
⅔ cup catsup
½ cup bottled smoke-flavor barbecue sauce
¼ cup light corn syrup

1 Have meatman crack ribs in half lengthwise to form long strips. Simmer strips, covered, in boiling salted water in a kettle 1 hour, or just until tender; drain.
2 When ready to grill, thread strips, accordion style, onto long skewers. Mix catsup, barbecue sauce, and corn syrup in a small saucepan; brush part over ribs; place on grill about 6 inches above hot coals.
3 Grill, turning and brushing often with remaining sauce, 20 minutes, or until richly glazed.

Mandarin Pork

Meat choice is country-style spareribs to cook on the rotisserie, then dunk in a tart fruit sauce.
Makes 4 servings

4 pounds country-style spareribs
Garlic salt
PLUM SAUCE *(recipe follows)*

1 Thread ribs on rotisserie spit, following manufacturer's directions; sprinkle with garlic salt. Set spit in position over hot coals; start rotisserie.
2 Cook, following manufacturer's directions, 1½ hours, or until meat is tender and richly browned.
3 Remove to a carving board; take out spit. Serve ribs with PLUM SAUCE.

PLUM SAUCE—Combine 1 cup plum jam with

1 tablespoon cider vinegar, 1 teaspoon grated onion, ½ teaspoon ground allspice, and ¼ teaspoon ground ginger in a small saucepan. Heat slowly, stirring constantly, to boiling. Serve warm or cold. Makes about 1 cup.

Halakahiki Veal Ribs
Pineapple two ways—juice and fruit—is the secret to their mellow flavor.
Bake at 350° for 2 hours. Makes 4 servings

4 *pounds breast of veal*
1 *can (6 ounces) frozen concentrate for pineapple-orange juice, thawed*
1 *can (about 9 ounces) crushed pineapple*
2 *teaspoons bottled aromatic bitters*

1 Cut breast of veal into pieces of 1 or 2 ribs each. Place in a single layer in a baking pan, 15x10x1.
2 Blend concentrate for pineapple-orange juice with pineapple and syrup and bitters in a small bowl; spoon over meat.
3 Bake in moderate oven (350°) 1½ hours; spoon juices from pan over meat. Continue baking, basting several times, 30 minutes, or until meat is tender and richly glazed.

Apricot-Glazed Ribs
A fruity sauce glazes veal as it spins on the rotisserie.
Makes 4 servings

4 *pounds breast of veal*
4 *teaspoons seasoned salt*
½ *cup sweet vermouth*
½ *cup vegetable oil*
½ *cup apricot nectar (from a 12-ounce can)*

1 Thread breast of veal, accordion style, onto rotisserie spit, following manufacturer's directions; sprinkle with seasoned salt. Set spit in position over hot coals; start rotisserie.
2 Mix vermouth and vegetable oil in a small saucepan; brush part over meat.
3 Cook, following manufacturer's directions, brushing several times with oil mixture, 1 hour and 45 minutes, or until meat is almost tender.
4 Stir apricot nectar into remaining oil mixture; brush over meat. Continue cooking, brushing several times with apricot mixture, 30 minutes, or until meat is tender and golden-brown. Remove to a carving board; take out spit. Cut ribs into serving-size pieces.

Tibetan Riblets
Cumin, coriander, and turmeric blend for an exotic flavor booster for lamb.
Makes 4 servings

4 *pounds breast of lamb*
2 *cartons (8 ounces each) plain yogurt*
1 *cup milk*
2 *tablespoons catsup*
1 *teaspoon cumin seeds*
1 *teaspoon coriander seeds, crushed*
½ *teaspoon turmeric*
½ *teaspoon ground ginger*
  Chopped fresh mint

1 Trim any excess fat from lamb. Cut lamb, if needed, into pieces of 1 or 2 ribs each; place in a large shallow dish.
2 Mix yogurt, milk, catsup, cumin seeds, coriander seeds, turmeric, and ginger in a small bowl; pour over ribs; turn pieces to coat well. Chill, turning several times, 2 hours to season.
3 When ready to grill, place ribs on a rack 4 inches above hot coals.
4 Grill about 2 hours or until tender and crispy-brown, turning and brushing often with remaining marinade. Before serving, sprinkle with chopped mint.

Tarragon Ribs
Simmer the meat first, then grill and serve with zippy horseradish sauce.
Makes 4 servings

4 *pounds beef short ribs*
2 *teaspoons salt*
1 *medium-size onion, peeled and sliced*
½ *cup (1 stick) butter or margarine*
2 *teaspoons dried tarragon leaves, crumbled*
1 *teaspoon liquid red pepper seasoning*
  HORSERADISH SAUCE *(recipe follows)*

1 Trim any excess fat from short ribs. Combine meat with salt and onion in a kettle or Dutch oven. Add water to cover; heat to boiling; cover.
2 Simmer 30 minutes; drain. Place ribs on grill about 10 inches from hot coals.
3 Melt butter or margarine in a small saucepan; stir in tarragon and red pepper seasoning; brush part over meat.
4 Grill, turning and brushing often with butter sauce, 1¼ hours, or until meat is tender and crispy-brown. Serve with HORSERADISH SAUCE.

COOKING OVER THE COALS

HORSERADISH SAUCE—Melt 2 tablespoons butter or margarine in a small saucepan; stir in 2 tablespoons flour and ½ teaspoon salt; cook, stirring constantly, just until bubbly. Stir in 1 cup light cream or table cream; continue cooking and stirring until sauce thickens and boils 1 minute; remove from heat. Stir in 2 tablespoons prepared horseradish. Makes about 1 cup.

●

Chef's Lamb Bake
Bottled salad dressing plus chili and steak sauces seasons the ribs simply but expertly. Bake at 350° for 1½ hours. Makes 4 servings

4 pounds breast of lamb
1 bottle (8 ounces) oil-and-vinegar salad dressing
1 cup bottled chili sauce
¼ cup bottled steak sauce

1 Trim any excess fat from lamb. Cut lamb, if needed, into pieces of 1 or 2 ribs each; place in a shallow dish.
2 Mix salad dressing and chili and steak sauces in a small bowl; pour over ribs; turn pieces to coat well. Chill, turning several times, 2 hours to season.
3 When ready to bake, place ribs on a rack in a large shallow baking pan.
4 Bake in moderate oven (350°), turning and brushing several times with sauce from dish, 1½ hours, or until meat is tender and crispy-brown.

●

All-Purpose Barbecue Sauce
Keep a jar on hand to use plain or to combine with extra seasonings called for in each kebab recipe.

Combine ½ cup light molasses, ½ cup catsup, 1 cup prepared mustard, and 1 cup cider vinegar in a 4-cup jar with tight-fitting cover. Shake to mix well. Store in the refrigerator. Makes 3 cups.

Gay kebab combo: Lamb and Bacon.

Herbed Lamb Ribs

Thrifty breast of lamb comes off the grill cooked sweetly tender right to the bone.
Makes 6 servings

    4 to 5 pounds breast of lamb
    2 cloves of garlic, sliced
    2 teaspoons salt
    ½ teaspoon pepper
        HERB BARBECUE SAUCE (recipe follows)

1 Cut lamb, if needed, into 5- to 6-inch-long strips, each about 3 inches wide.
2 Place in large kettle with water to cover; add garlic, salt, and pepper. Cover; simmer 15 to 20 minutes, or just until barely tender; drain. (This much can be done ahead, if you like.)
3 Thread lamb on long skewers; brush with HERB BARBECUE SAUCE.
4 Grill over hot coals, turning and brushing often with sauce, 1 hour, or until richly glazed and meat is tender enough almost to fall off bones.

   HERB BARBECUE SAUCE—Combine 1 cup ALL-PURPOSE BARBECUE SAUCE (recipe precedes); ½ cup chili sauce; and ½ teaspoon rosemary, crushed, in small saucepan. Makes 1½ cups.

Green-and-Yellow Kebabs

Vegetables take to kebab cooking, too. Here cucumbers join with squashes.
Makes 6 servings

    3 medium-size cucumbers
    3 medium-size yellow squashes
    ½ cup bottled Italian salad dressing

1 Trim ends of cucumbers and squashes, but do not pare. Cut each into 1-inch-thick slices.
2 Place in single layer in large shallow pan or use 2 large frying pans; add water to depth of ½ inch; cover; parboil 3 minutes; drain.
3 Thread, alternating cucumber and squash slices, through skin onto long skewers; brush with Italian salad dressing.
4 Grill over hot coals, turning and brushing often with sauce, 20 minutes, or until tender and glazed.

Liver-and-Bacon Kebabs

A favorite pair—liver and bacon—grill perfectly out-of-doors. Here's how.
Makes 4 servings

    8 small white onions
    1 pound beef, lamb, or calf's liver, thinly sliced
    4 slices bacon

    1 large sweet red pepper, seeded and cut into 12 squares
    1 large green pepper, seeded and cut into 12 squares
        ZIPPY BARBECUE SAUCE (recipe follows)

1 Peel onions; parboil in boiling salted water in small saucepan 5 minutes; drain. (Save for Step 3.)
2 Cut liver slices into strips about the width of sliced bacon. Lay bacon strips on a board; top each with 1 or 2 strips of liver.
3 Thread each of 4 long skewers in this order: One onion; 3 squares of peppers (mixed red and green); liver-and-bacon, laced accordion style onto skewer; 3 pepper squares; and 1 onion. Brush with ZIPPY BARBECUE SAUCE.
4 Grill over hot coals, turning and brushing often with sauce, 15 minutes, or just until bacon is crisp. Do not overcook, for it will toughen liver. Time will depend on heat of coals and distance of kebabs from heat.

   ZIPPY BARBECUE SAUCE—Combine 1 cup ALL-PURPOSE BARBECUE SAUCE (recipe precedes), ¼ cup catsup, ¼ cup vegetable oil, and 2 tablespoons Worcestershire sauce in small saucepan. Makes about 1½ cups.

Teriyaki Sticks

Thin strips of spicy-seasoned round steak, shrimps, and fresh pineapple make these exotic kebabs.
Makes 6 servings

    1 piece top round beef steak, weighing about 1¾ pounds and cut 1¼ inches thick
    ¼ cup frozen concentrated pineapple juice (from a 6-ounce can)
    ¼ cup water
    2 tablespoons olive oil
    1 tablespoon bottled meat sauce
    1 clove garlic, crushed
    1 teaspoon ground ginger
    ½ teaspoon anise seeds, crushed
    12 frozen deveined shelled raw shrimps, thawed
    2 one-inch-thick slices fresh pineapple, pared, cored, and cut in 9 wedges each

1 Pierce steak deeply all over with a fork; place in a shallow dish.
2 Mix concentrated pineapple juice, water, olive oil, meat sauce, garlic, ginger, and anise seeds in a 1-cup measure; pour over steak; cover. Chill, turning steak once, 30 minutes; remove from marinade to a cutting board; discard marinade.

3 Cut meat diagonally into long slices about ¼ inch thick; thread, accordion style, with 2 shrimps and 3 pineapple wedges onto each of 6 long skewers. Place on grill about 6 inches above hot coals.

4 Grill, turning once, 6 minutes for rare, or until steak is done as you like it.

Shrimps Pacifica
Perfect finger fare! Everybody shells his own shrimps, then dips them into a spunky sauce. Makes 4 servings

 1 pound large raw shrimps in shell
 ½ cup peanut oil or vegetable oil
 ½ cup lemon juice
 1 teaspoon Italian seasoning
 1 teaspoon seasoned salt
 ½ teaspoon seasoned pepper
 2 tablespoons brown sugar
 1 teaspoon soy sauce
 ¼ cup thinly sliced green onions

1 Wash shrimps under cold running water; remove feelers but do not shell; drain on paper toweling. Place in a medium-size bowl.

2 Stir in peanut oil or vegetable oil, lemon juice, Italian seasoning, and seasoned salt and pepper. Let stand, turning several times, 30 minutes.

3 Lift shrimps from marinade with a slotted spoon and place on grill about 6 inches from hot coals; brush with marinade. Grill, turning once and brushing with more marinade, 10 minutes, or until shrimps are tender.

4 Pour remaining marinade into a small saucepan; stir in brown sugar and soy sauce. Heat to boiling, then stir in green onions. Serve separately as a dip.

714

Veal Mixed Grill
Here's showy outdoor cooking with peppy-seasoned veal kebabs, spicy sausages, and savory eggplant-tomato stacks. Makes 6 servings

1½ pounds veal shoulder, cut in 1½-inch cubes
     Instant unseasoned meat tenderizer
 ½ cup mayonnaise or salad dressing
 ¼ cup unsweetened grapefruit juice
 2 tablespoons Worcestershire sauce
 1 clove of garlic, minced
 1 teaspoon paprika
 1 teaspoon celery salt

 ¼ teaspoon hickory smoked salt
 6 small pork sausage links (about ½ pound)
 3 medium-size tomatoes, halved crosswise
 1 small eggplant, pared and sliced ½ inch thick
 4 tablespoons (½ stick) butter or margarine
     Salt and pepper

1 Moisten veal and sprinkle with tenderizer, following label directions. Thread onto 6 skewers.

2 Blend mayonnaise or salad dressing, grapefruit juice, Worcestershire sauce, garlic, paprika, celery salt, and hickory smoked salt in a small bowl. Brush over veal cubes.

3 Place skewers on grill about 4 inches from hot coals. Grill, turning often and brushing with more sauce, 25 minutes, or until tender.

4 While veal cooks, place sausages in a small frying pan; prick skins slightly with a fork. Place on grill. Cook, turning once or twice, 15 to 20 minutes, or until well browned.

5 Brush tomatoes and both sides of eggplant slices with melted butter or margarine; sprinkle with salt and pepper. Place in a single layer on a sheet of foil on grill. (Turn edges of foil up to keep juices from running out.) Cook, turning eggplant once, 10 minutes, or until eggplant is tender and tomatoes are hot.

6 When ready to serve, place skewered veal and sausages in center of a large platter. Place eggplant around edge; top with tomato halves.

Indonesian Beef en Brochette
Best-buy chuck is the meat choice; coriander and cumin add the unusual seasoning twist. Makes 4 servings

 1 piece chuck beef steak, weighing about 2½ pounds and cut 1½ inches thick
 ½ cup soy sauce
 ½ cup lemon juice
 2 tablespoons brown sugar
 2 teaspoons ground coriander
 2 teaspoons ground cumin
1½ teaspoons salt
 1 teaspoon pepper
 1 large onion, peeled and sliced
     Instant unseasoned meat tenderizer
 8 small white onions, peeled

1 Trim all fat from steak, then cut meat into 1½-inch cubes; pierce all over with a fork. Place in a large shallow dish.

2 Mix soy sauce, lemon juice, brown sugar, coriander, cumin, salt, pepper, and sliced onion in a small bowl; pour over meat. Chill, turning several times, 30 minutes.

3 Remove meat from marinade; set marinade

Because meats and vegetables grill at different speeds, it's best to skewer and cook them separately.

Charcoal grilling at home or away is really child's play. Once the coals are white-hot, easy does it!

aside. Sprinkle meat with tenderizer, following label directions; let stand 30 minutes.

4 Parboil small onions in boiling salted water in a small saucepan 5 minutes; drain.

5 Thread 4 cubes of meat and 2 small onions onto each of 4 long skewers. Place on grill about 6 inches above hot coals.

6 Grill, turning and brushing several times with saved marinade, 20 minutes for rare, or until meat is done as you like it. Sprinkle onions with paprika, if you wish.

Herbed Vegetable Kebabs
Potatoes, two kinds of squashes, tomatoes, mushrooms, and green pepper take to skewer-cooking like a dream.
Makes 4 servings

8 small new potatoes
2 medium-size zucchini

715

2 medium-size yellow squashes
8 large fresh mushrooms
2 large tomatoes
1 large green pepper
4 tablespoons (½ stick) butter or margarine
2 teaspoons fines herbes

1 Scrub potatoes; cut off a band of skin around middle of each. Trim zucchini and yellow squashes but do not pare; cut each in 1-inch-thick slices.
2 Parboil potatoes in boiling salted water in a medium-size saucepan 15 minutes; drain. Parboil squashes together in boiling salted water in a second medium-size saucepan 5 minutes; drain.
3 While potatoes and squashes cook, wash mushrooms, trim ends, and halve each. Cut each tomato in 8 wedges. Halve green pepper; remove seeds; cut pepper in ¼-inch-wide strips. Thread potatoes and squashes, alternately, onto each of 4 long skewers; thread mushrooms, tomato wedges, and green-pepper strips, alternately, onto each of 4 more long skewers.
4 Melt butter or margarine in a small saucepan; stir in fines herbes; brush part over vegetables.
5 Place squash and potato skewers on grill about 6 inches above hot coals. Grill, turning and brushing several times with more butter mixture, 10 minutes; place mushroom-tomato skewers alongside.
6 Continue grilling all 10 minutes, or until potatoes and squashes are tender and mushrooms and tomatoes are heated through.

Pork on-a-Stick
New instant meat marinade is the seasoner and tenderizer for these husky kebabs.
Makes 6 servings

2 pounds lean fresh pork shoulder, cut in 1-inch cubes
1 envelope instant meat marinade
Water
6 whole spiced crab apples (from a 1-pound jar)

1 Place pork cubes in a shallow dish. Prepare instant meat marinade with water, following label directions; pour over pork; pierce cubes all over with a fork. Let stand, turning meat often, 15 minutes.
2 When ready to cook, thread cubes, allowing about a half inch between each, onto 6 long skewers; place on grill about 6 inches above hot coals. Pour marinade into a small saucepan.

3 Grill, turning and brushing once or twice with remaining marinade, 40 minutes, or until pork is tender and richly glazed. Place a crab apple on the end of each skewer.

All-American Beef Roll Roast
For a party, it can't be beat. For the family, it's holiday fare.
Makes 12 to 16 servings

Buy an about-6-pound piece of rolled boneless eye round or a 4-rib roast of beef, boned and rolled. (Be sure to ask for the rib bones to simmer for making soup or gravy.) Rub meat well with a mixture of 2 tablespoons flour, 1 teaspoon seasoned salt, and ¼ teaspoon seasoned pepper. Place on rotisserie spit, following manufacturer's directions. If using a meat thermometer, insert bulb deeply into one end of meat so spit can turn. Set spit in position over hot coals; start rotisserie. Roast, following manufacturer's directions, 1½ hours for rare, or until thermometer registers 140°. Count on about 20 minutes longer for medium, or 160°. Remove meat to carving board with a well to catch juices; take out spit. Slice meat; spoon juices over.

Over-the-Coals Corned Beef
Simmer meat until tender, then glaze on your outdoor grill. Have big buttered buns ready to make into sandwiches.
Makes 12 servings

5 pounds corned-beef brisket
1 medium-size onion, sliced
1 tablespoon mixed pickling spices
¼ cup prepared mustard
2 tablespoons brown sugar
¼ teaspoon nutmeg
⅛ teaspoon freshly ground black pepper

1 Simmer corned beef with onion and pickling spices in water to cover in a kettle 3 hours, or until tender. Let stand in broth until ready to glaze.
2 Brush meat all over with about half of the mustard. Mix remaining mustard with brown sugar, nutmeg, and pepper in a cup; save for next step. Place meat on grill over hot coals.
3 Grill 15 minutes; turn; grill 15 minutes longer. Brush half of mustard mixture over meat; turn again and grill 15 minutes. Brush with remaining mustard mixture; turn again and grill 15 minutes longer, or until crusty-brown. (Time will depend on how hot coals are and the distance of meat from coals.)
4 Remove meat to cutting board; slice across the grain.

The list of charcoal grillables goes on and on, includes giant roasts, steaks, chops and vegetables.

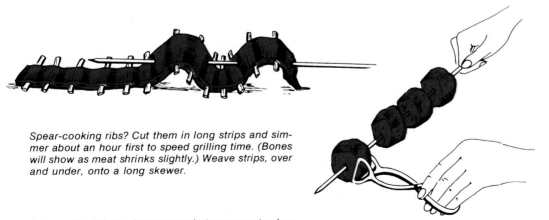

Spear-cooking ribs? Cut them in long strips and simmer about an hour first to speed grilling time. (Bones will show as meat shrinks slightly.) Weave strips, over and under, onto a long skewer.

In threading kebabs, leave space between meat cubes so they'll brown on all sides. Tongs are handy helpers if meat has been marinated.

A round-up of all-time charcoal grill hits: hotdogs, these bacon-wrapped and stuffed with crisp scallions; a giant sirloin pounded with crushed peppercorns; half young broiler-fryers and skewersful of ribs.

718

Outdoor Lamb Roasts

Simmer lamb shanks until tender indoors, then glaze them sparkly-brown over the coals.
Makes 4 servings

4 lamb shanks
1 teaspoon leaf rosemary, crumbled
2 teaspoons salt
1 small onion, chopped (¼ cup)
4 cups water
½ cup bottled barbecue sauce
½ cup catsup

1 Place lamb shanks, rosemary, salt, onion, and water in a large saucepan. Heat to boiling, then simmer 1 hour, or until tender; drain. (If cooked ahead, chill, then remove from refrigerator about 30 minutes before grilling.)
2 Place lamb on grill about 6 inches from hot coals. Combine barbecue sauce and catsup in a small saucepan; brush over lamb to coat generously. Grill, turning once and brushing often with more sauce, 20 minutes, or until richly glazed.

Barbecued Veal Roast

For showy outdoor cooking with a thrifty price tag, watch for a special on a shoulder roast.
Makes 8 to 10 servings

2 slices bacon, halved
1 rolled boneless veal shoulder roast, weighing about 5 pounds
½ cup (1 stick) butter or margarine
1 cup catsup
2 tablespoons cider vinegar
1 tablespoon Worcestershire sauce
1 teaspoon salt
½ teaspoon leaf basil, crumbled
¼ teaspoon leaf thyme, crumbled
¼ teaspoon freshly ground pepper
3 tablespoons brown sugar

1 Push two pieces of bacon into each end of veal roast, cutting a slit in meat, if necessary.
2 Place meat on spit, following manufacturer's directions. If using a meat thermometer, insert bulb in end of roast to center without touching spit. Set spit in position over hot coals; start rotisserie. Roast 1½ hours.
3 While meat roasts, melt butter or margarine in a small saucepan; stir in remaining ingredients, except brown sugar; simmer, stirring several times, 5 minutes. Brush part over meat.
4 Continue roasting, basting every half hour with more sauce, 1 hour, or until thermometer registers 170° and meat is tender and richly glazed.
5 Remove to a cutting board; take out spit.
6 Stir brown sugar into remaining sauce; heat on side of grill until hot. Carve roast into ¼-inch-thick slices; serve with sauce to spoon over top.

Chicken for a Crowd
Allow plenty of cooking time, for the meat should almost fall off the bones.
Makes 12 servings

6 broiler-fryers, split (1½ to 2 pounds each)
2 cups vegetable oil

For a huge crowd, a whole loin can be split-roasted. Best choices are young pig or lamb.

½ cup lime or lemon juice
2 teaspoons salt
¼ cup honey

1 Wash chicken halves, then dry. Mix vegetable oil, lime or lemon juice, and salt in a small saucepan; brush part over chickens. Place, skin side up, on grill about 6 inches above hot coals.
2 Grill, turning and brushing often with more sauce, 1 hour.
3 Stir honey into remaining sauce; brush over chickens. Continue grilling, turning often and brushing with remaining sauce, 15 minutes, or until golden-brown and joints move easily.

Whirlybird Roast

Currant jelly glazes the chicken as it spins on the rotisserie.
Makes 4 to 6 servings

2 cups ready-mix bread stuffing
½ cup (1 stick) butter or margarine, melted
⅔ cup water
1 four-pound roasting chicken
½ cup currant jelly, melted

1 Prepare stuffing mix with ⅓ cup of the melted butter or margarine and water, following label directions.
2 Wash chicken, then dry. Stuff neck and body cavities lightly; skewer neck skin to body; tie legs tightly to tail.
3 Place chicken on spit, following manufacturer's directions; brush with remaining melted butter or margarine. Set spit in position over hot coals; start rotisserie.
4 Roast, following manufacturer's directions, 1 hour; brush with melted jelly. Continue roasting, brushing often with more jelly, 15 minutes longer, or until chicken is tender and richly glazed.

Island Turkey Roast

720

Meat sizzles away in a spicy fruit sauce inside its foil wrapper.
Makes 8 to 10 servings

1 frozen rolled boneless turkey roast (about 4 pounds), thawed
1 can (about 9 ounces) crushed pineapple, well drained
¼ cup honey
1 teaspoon ground cinnamon
½ teaspoon curry powder
½ teaspoon garlic salt

1 Place turkey roast in center of a large sheet of heavy foil. (Sheet should be large enough to cover roast loosely with triple folds at top and ends.)
2 Mix remaining ingredients in a small bowl; spread over turkey to cover completely. Wrap loosely but seal tightly. Set package on grill over very hot coals. (You will need a fire bed big enough to last about 2½ hours.)
3 Roast, turning every 30 minutes, from 35 to 40 minutes per pound, or about 2½ hours. (If you wish to test roast with a meat thermometer, insert bulb through foil into center of roast after last turning. This keeps juices from running out. When meat is done, thermometer should register 185°.)
4 Remove package from grill; slit foil across top; place turkey on a cutting board. Cover; let stand 20 minutes for easier carving.
5 Pour juices from package into a small saucepan; heat to boiling. Slice turkey; spoon juices over.

Stuffed Hot-Dog Wieners

Each sizzly-hot bacon-wrapped wiener is stuffed with a snappy green onion.
Makes 8 servings

1 can (8 ounces) tomato sauce
1 tablespoon instant coffee powder
1 tablespoon sugar
8 frankfurters (about 1 pound)
8 green onions, trimmed
8 slices bacon

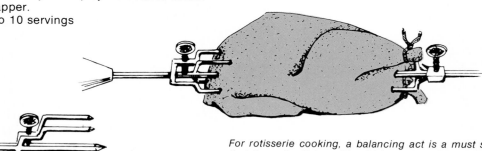

For rotisserie cooking, a balancing act is a must so that the spit will turn. Tie chicken—or turkey—tightly with string to make a compact roast, then mount it right in the middle of the spit.

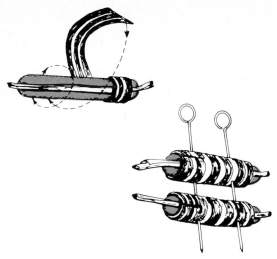

Bacon slice goes round and round a plump wiener to hold in the nippy onion stuffer. For easy turning, string two or more franks on a pair of metal skewers.

1 Mix tomato sauce, instant coffee, and sugar in a small saucepan.
2 Split each frankfurter lengthwise; brush inside with part of the sauce mixture, then place a green onion in each. Wrap with a bacon slice; fasten with wooden picks. Place on grill about 6 inches above hot coals. (Soak picks in water first to keep them from charring.)
3 Grill, turning and brushing often with more sauce, 20 minutes, or until bacon is crisp. Serve in toasted frankfurter rolls, if you wish.

Glazed Coneys

Grill wieners until plump and sparkling, pop into a toasty bun, and dig in!
Makes 8 servings

8 frankfurters (about 1 pound)
2 tablespoons prepared mustard
2 tablespoons molasses
2 tablespoons cider vinegar
1 teaspoon Worcestershire sauce
1 teaspoon vegetable oil
8 split frankfurter rolls, toasted and buttered

1 Score frankfurters in crisscross cuts about ¼ inch deep.
2 Mix mustard, molasses, vinegar, Worcestershire sauce, and vegetable oil in a small saucepan; brush part over frankfurters; place on grill about 6 inches above hot coals.
3 Grill, turning and brushing once or twice with more sauce, 12 minutes, or until richly glazed. Serve in toasted rolls.

TWO GOURMET FEASTS FROM THE GRILL

Antipasto on a Skewer
Lime Cooler
Whirlybird Stuffed Ham
Dilled Rice Bake
Molded Carrot Cups
Little Corn Loaves
Cherry Cream Pie
with Brandied Peach Sauce

Lime Cooler

Makes 12 servings, about 1 cup each

1 can (6 ounces) frozen concentrate for red Hawaiian punch
2 cans (6 ounces each) frozen concentrate for limeade
12 cups water
Ice cubes

1 Mix Hawaiian punch, limeade, and water in a kettle.
2 Just before serving, pour over ice in tall glasses. Garnish each with a sprig of mint.

Antipasto on a Skewer

Makes 12 servings

¾ cup olive oil
¼ cup wine vinegar
½ teaspoon salt
½ teaspoon sugar
½ teaspoon dry mustard
½ teaspoon leaf oregano, crumbled
¼ teaspoon pepper
1 package (8 ounces) mozzarella cheese
1 package (4 ounces) sliced salami
24 cherry tomatoes
12 small mushrooms, trimmed
1 jar (6 ounces) marinated artichoke hearts
24 pitted ripe olives

1 Combine olive oil, vinegar, salt, sugar, mustard, oregano, and pepper in a jar with a tight lid; shake well to mix.
2 Cut mozzarella cheese in thick slices, then cut slices lengthwise into sticks. Wrap each stick inside a slice of salami; cut in half crosswise; fasten each half with a wooden pick.
3 Thread 2 tomatoes, 1 mushroom, 1 artichoke heart, 3 salami rolls, and 2 olives onto each of 12 long skewers; place in a large shallow baking dish. Drizzle dressing over top. Let stand about an hour to season and blend flavors.
4 Lift skewers from dressing; arrange on a large serving tray.

721

Whirlybird Stuffed Ham
Makes 12 generous servings

6 pounds boned rolled ready-to-eat ham
1 cup chopped escarole
1 cup chopped parsley
¼ cup finely cut chives
½ cup honey
½ cup cranberry-orange relish (from a 14-ounce jar)

1 Stand ham upright on a cutting board. Snip off end clip, if any, but leave wrapping on while fixing meat. To make cavities for stuffing, work rotisserie spit through ham in 4 places, then enlarge each hole with a wooden-spoon handle.
2 Mix escarole, parsley, and chives in a medium-size bowl; stuff about ½ cup of the greens mixture into each hole, packing it in firmly with wooden-spoon handle. Peel wrapping from ham.
3 Place ham on spit, following manufacturer's directions; set spit in position over hot coals; start rotisserie. Roast 1½ hours.
4 Mix honey and cranberry-orange relish in a small saucepan; heat to boiling; brush a small amount over ham. Continue roasting, brushing every 15 minutes with more honey mixture, 1½ hours, or until ham is richly glazed.
5 Remove ham to a carving board; take out spit. Drizzle any remaining sauce over ham. Carve in ¼-inch-thick slices.

Dilled Rice Bake
Bake at 350° for 40 minutes. Makes 12 servings

2 cups regular uncooked rice
3 eggs
1 carton (1 pound) cream-style cottage cheese
1 medium-size cucumber, pared, quartered, and sliced thin
1½ cups milk
2 tablespoons chopped fresh dill
2 teaspoons salt
¼ teaspoon pepper

1 Cook rice, following label directions.
2 Beat eggs slightly in a large bowl. Stir in cottage cheese, cucumber, milk, dill, salt, and pepper; fold in hot rice. Spoon into a 12-cup baking dish.
3 Bake in moderate oven (350°) 40 minutes,

or until set. Just before serving, garnish with several fronds of fresh dill and cucumber slices, if you wish.

Molded Carrot Cups
Makes 12 servings

2 packages (6 ounces each) lemon-flavor gelatin
4 cups boiling water
2 cups cold water
½ cup cider vinegar
¾ cup finely diced green pepper
2 cups shredded carrots
Chicory or curly endive
Mayonnaise or salad dressing

1 Dissolve gelatin in boiling water in a large bowl; stir in cold water and vinegar. Measure 1½ cups of mixture into a small bowl for next step. Keep remaining gelatin mixture at room temperature while layering molds.
2 Place small bowl in a pan of ice and water to speed setting. Chill until as thick as unbeaten egg white; fold in green pepper. Spoon into 12 five-ounce custard cups. Chill in refrigerator just until sticky-firm.
3 While molds chill, place bowl of remaining gelatin mixture in ice and water. Chill just until as thick as unbeaten egg white; fold in carrots. Spoon over pepper layers in molds. Chill at least 4 hours, or until firm. (Overnight is best.)
4 When ready to serve, unmold onto salad plates. Garnish with chicory or curly endive and top each with mayonnaise or salad dressing.

Little Corn Loaves
Bake at 400° for 20 minutes. Makes 12 small loaves

2 packages (14 ounces each) corn muffin mix
2 teaspoons leaf basil, crumbled
Eggs
Milk
2 tablespoons butter or margarine, melted

1 Grease 12 loaf pans, 4½x2½x1½.
2 Combine corn muffin mix and basil in a large bowl; add eggs and milk. Mix, following label directions. Spoon into prepared pans, dividing evenly. Set pans in a jelly-roll pan for easy handling.
3 Bake in hot oven (400°) 20 minutes, or until

Whirlybird Stuffed Ham: a boned and rolled ham, polka-dotted with parsley and chives and grilled

722

firm and golden. Remove from pans to wire racks. Brush with melted butter or margarine; serve warm.

Note—If loaves are made ahead, reheat just before serving this way: Brush each with melted butter or margarine, wrap in foil, and heat on side of grill. If you do not have small loaf pans, bake batter in muffin-pan cups, following directions on muffin-mix package.

To end a grilled meal: cool, satiny Cherry Cream Pie.

Cherry Cream Pie
with Brandied Peach Sauce

Bake shell at 425° for 15 minutes. Makes 12 servings

½ package piecrust mix
½ gallon cherry-vanilla ice cream
1 cup sugar
¼ cup cornstarch
1 can (1 pound, 13 ounces) cling-peach slices
1 cup water
¼ cup brandy

1 Prepare piecrust mix, following label directions, or make pastry from your favorite single-crust recipe. Roll out to a 12-inch round on a lightly floured pastry cloth or board; fit into a 9-inch pie plate. Trim overhang to ½ inch; turn under, flush with rim; flute to make a stand-up edge. Prick shell well all over with a fork.
2 Bake in hot oven (425°) 15 minutes, or until pastry is golden; cool completely in pie plate on a wire rack.
3 Soften ice cream slightly in a large bowl; spoon into pastry shell. Freeze several hours, or overnight, until very firm.

724

4 Mix sugar and cornstarch in a large saucepan. Drain syrup from peaches and stir into cornstarch mixture with water; cook, stirring constantly, until sauce thickens and boils 3 minutes. Stir in peaches; heat just until hot; remove from heat. Stir in brandy.
5 Cut pie into thin wedges; spoon warm peach sauce over each.

●

TERRACE TRIUMPH
Cheese Toasties
Napoli Chicken Broil
Baked-Potato Bundles
Apple Scallop
Corn Combinage
Strawberry Torte

Cheese Toasties

Bake at 375° for 20 minutes. Makes 8 servings, 3 each

½ loaf unsliced firm white bread
4 tablespoons (½ stick) butter or margarine, melted
1 jar (5 ounces) process sharp Cheddar cheese spread
8 pimiento-stuffed olives, sliced

1 Trim crusts from bread; cut bread into 4 one-inch-thick slices; cut each slice into 6 small rectangles. Cut a small hollow in center of each rectangle with the tip of a small knife.
2 Brush rectangles all over with melted butter or margarine; place on a large cookie sheet.
3 Bake in moderate oven (375°) 10 minutes; remove from oven. Spoon cheese into hollows.
4 Bake 10 minutes longer, or until toasty-brown. Garnish each with a slice of olive.

Napoli Chicken Broil

Makes 8 servings

1 cup (2 sticks) butter or margarine
2 envelopes Italian-flavor salad dressing mix
¼ cup lime juice
8 chicken breasts, weighing about 12 ounces each

1 Melt butter or margarine in a small saucepan; stir in salad dressing mix and lime juice. Brush part over both sides of chicken.
2 Place chicken, skin side down, on grill about 10 inches above hot coals. Grill, turning and brushing pieces often with more butter mixture, 40 minutes, or until tender and richly glazed.

Baked-Potato Bundles
Makes 8 servings

8 medium-size baking potatoes, scrubbed and
   dried
   Vegetable oil
½ cup (1 stick) butter or margarine
1 teaspoon mixed salad herbs
3 tablespoons bacon-flavor bits

1 Rub each potato with vegetable oil; wrap in
a square of double-thick foil. Cook directly on
the coals or on top of the grill, turning several
times, 1 hour, or until soft when pressed with
fingers. (Protect fingers with a potholder.)
2 While potatoes bake, blend butter or margarine with salad herbs and bacon bits in a small
bowl; chill.
3 Unwrap each potato and fold foil back to form
a serving dish. Make a crisscross cut in top of
each potato, then squeeze firmly at both ends
to fluff up. Top with butter mixture.

Apple Scallop
Bake at 375° for 30 minutes. Makes 8 servings

2 cans (1 pound, 4 ounces each) pie-sliced
   apples
1 teaspoon ground cinnamon
½ teaspoon ground nutmeg
2 teaspoons lemon juice
1 cup sifted all-purpose flour
½ cup firmly packed brown sugar
½ cup (1 stick) butter or margarine
1 cup golden raisins

1 Combine apples, cinnamon, nutmeg, and
lemon juice in a large bowl; toss lightly to mix.
2 Mix flour and brown sugar in a medium-size
bowl; cut in butter or margarine with a pastry
blender until mixture is crumbly.
3 Spoon half of the apple mixture into an 8-cup
baking dish; sprinkle with half each of the raisins
and crumb mixture; repeat layers.
4 Bake in moderate oven (375°) 30 minutes,
or until golden. Serve hot as a relish.

Corn Combinage
Makes 8 servings

4 tablespoons (½ stick) butter or margarine
4 medium-size zucchini, sliced thin
1 teaspoon salt

¼ teaspoon pepper
¼ teaspoon leaf oregano, crumbled
2 cans (12 ounces each) Mexican-style corn

1 Melt butter or margarine in a large frying pan
on grill over hot coals. Stir in zucchini; sprinkle
with salt, pepper, and oregano. Sauté, stirring
several times, 5 minutes; push to one side.
2 Add corn to pan; cover. Simmer 5 minutes,
or until bubbly.

Strawberry Torte
Makes 12 servings

1 package orange chiffon cake mix
1 package (6 ounces) strawberry-flavor gelatin
2 cups boiling water
1 cup cold water
¼ cup lemon juice
1 jar (12 ounces) strawberry preserves
1 container (9 ounces) frozen whipped topping, thawed

1 Prepare cake mix, bake in a 10-inch tube cake
pan, cool, and remove from pan, following label
directions. Split cake into 4 even layers with a
sharp knife.
2 Dissolve gelatin in boiling water in a large
bowl; stir in cold water and lemon juice, then
strawberry preserves until well blended. Measure out 1 cup of the mixture; set aside.
3 Set large bowl of gelatin mixture in a pan of
ice and water to speed setting. Chill, stirring
several times, until slightly thickened. Beat in
2 cups of the whipped topping; continue chilling, stirring often, until mixture mounds on a
spoon.
4 Place bottom cake layer on a large serving
plate; spread with 1½ cups of the thickened
gelatin mixture, filling in center. Stack the two
middle layers, spreading each with 1½ cups
gelatin mixture, on top of bottom layer; cover
with top layer. Spoon any remaining gelatin
mixture into center. Chill while preparing frosting.
5 Pour the 1 cup gelatin mixture into same
bowl; beat in remaining 2 cups whipped topping; place over ice and water. Chill, stirring
several times, until mixture mounds on a spoon.
Spread over side and top of cake.
6 Chill several hours, or until frosting is firm.
Garnish with fresh strawberries, if you wish. Cut
into wedges.

725

COUNTDOWN ON CALORIES

**COUNTDOWN ON CALORIES:
THE COMMON SENSE OF COUNTING CALORIES, RULES OF REDUCING, DIET PLANS FOR ADULTS AND TEENAGERS, WEIGHTLESS DINNER, COUNTDOWN DESSERTS**

You will find it helpful, if you are to control your weight successfully, to understand as much as you can about your own particular problem. Think about yourself a little. Why did you gain? When did you gain? How long has it taken those creeping ounces to become pounds? How much should you weigh? How can you lose? How can you reach the weight you want and keep it? If your other diet attempts have failed, what can make another one work?

THE COMMON SENSE OF COUNTING CALORIES

Are you overeating?
Start by accepting the fact that one natural law of weight control applies to you and to everyone else:

If more fuel than the body can use for energy is consistently taken in, the excess will be stored as fat and weight will be gained. If consistently the body gets less fuel than it needs for activity and to keep itself going, body fat will be burned and weight will be lost.

Can you believe these lavish desserts are low-calorie?

If you can firmly believe that this is true, the knowledge will stand by you steadfastly while you work at your own weight-control program. This principle helps as well in understanding your weight problem:

If you gain weight, you are somehow eating too much or burning up too little fuel.

What makes you overeat?
Few of us eat too much on purpose. There are other factors at work—and paying some attention to them can in many cases help us stop gaining and even let us start to lose. Ask yourself some questions:

• *Is relaxation my downfall?* Relaxation encourages eating. Even an extra 25 calories (a few peanuts, for example) a day can cause a person to gain up to two pounds a year.

• *Do I overeat when I'm tense?* In times of stress it's natural to turn to food as a tranquilizer or a pacifier.

• *Do I snack when I'm bored?* Sometimes it seems easier to eat than to act. Both eating and lassitude can contribute to overweight.

• *Have I maintained food intake as I've added birthdays?* After age 25 (the time when the body is fully developed) calorie needs diminish. If food intake remains the same, and particularly if activity slackens, added years mean added pounds.

• *Do I simply enjoy good food?* If you're a good cook and enjoy cooking and eating, you can overeat simply out of pleasure. With good food abundant and easy to prepare, temptation surrounds us.

• *Do I eat when I feel tired?* We can mistake for hunger pangs the body's need for rest, for a change of pace, for exercise.

• *Am I from a "fat" family?* There is some evidence that heredity can play a part in a tendency of some persons to gain weight. In other "fat" families there simply is a tradition of overeating. In either case, you as an individual can control your weight with careful dieting and exercise.

• *Do I have a health problem?* Weight gain is associated with a number of health problems; a checkup by your doctor to find out your health status should be the starting point of your weight-control program.

• *Do I eat the right things?* You may overeat without getting all the nutrients your body needs to be well fed. A weight-control diet should supply all your daily food needs except calories. Good nutrition will help appease your appetite.

• *Have I decreased my activity?* Count up your household conveniences—each one saves body fuel. If you slack off on activity, you should also slack off on food intake. Stepping up your activity can on the other hand help you control weight.

When did you gain?

Some women will say they've always been overweight. Others know they gained at a specific time. Understanding the circumstances in which you gained any extra weight may help get you back in control.

• *Are you gaining now?* If you are in the 25-to-35 or the 55-to-65 age bracket, it may help to be aware that these are danger zones in weight control. Take into account that as your daily calorie needs are diminishing, you are perhaps less active than you once were. Cut your food intake accordingly. Just giving up little extras— cream and sugar in coffee, for example—helps, but may not be enough. Watching calorie intake and cutting out second helpings can stop the steady weight gains that could one day add up to obesity.

• *Did you gain when you got married?* Cooking for a husband has made many a slim bride fat. The pitfalls are tasting too much as you cook, eating leftovers just because they're there, eating to encourage others to eat, or appreciation of your own cooking.

• *Did you gain with a pregnancy?* Many women

gain when they're having a baby and never seem able to get rid of those extra pounds. Sometimes, however, a pregnancy masks creeping overweight that is recognized only when it doesn't dissolve after the baby comes. Doctors today encourage women to hold to a minimum any weight gain during pregnancy and to get back into their prepregnancy clothes within a month or so after delivery.

• *Did you gain as a teenager?* During adolescence a girl often puts on pounds. Usually doctors take this rounding out matter-of-factly, because a girl usually slims down again as she reaches her full height and her body adjusts into womanhood. Sometimes, however, the extra roundness stays. In your early 20s, you should be at your normal—and *best*—weight.

• *Have you always been overweight?* If so, you probably are accustomed to overeating and underexercising. Habitual overeating—or heredity or some health factor—may have set your appetite-control too high. Long-term diet control can help you adjust it to a lower food demand.

THE RULES OF REDUCING

1 The more overweight you are, the faster you should reduce.

2 The smaller your overweight, the slower you should reduce.

3 The older you are, the smaller the calorie deficit should be. This gives the skin of older people more time to shrink without sagging or developing wrinkles.

4 If you are a young adult, you will do better on a more drastic diet.

5 Eat only the foods and the amounts of food recommended by your doctor or allowed by your diet.

6 Don't cheat!

7 Prepare or have your food prepared without added butter or margarine, fat, sugar or flour.

8 Eat your salads plain or dressed with vinegar, lemon juice, salt, pepper and mustard. No oils!

9 Drink all the water you want.

10 Salt your food as you wish unless instructed otherwise by your doctor.

11 Satisfy your between-meals' hunger with a no-calorie appetite appeaser such as a chunk of celery, a carrot stick, a cup of tea or coffee *minus* the cream and sugar.

12 Follow your diet to the letter, then when off the diet, continue to watch the calories carefully.

TABLE I

NORMAL WEIGHT FOR MEN OF SMALL, MEDIUM, AND LARGE FRAME [1]

(Weight and height as ordinarily dressed but without shoes, coat, and vest.)

Height [2]	Small Frame	Medium Frame	Large Frame
5'0''	118	126	134
5'1''	121	129	137
5'2''	124	132	140
5'3''	127	135	143
5'4''	131	139	147
5'5''	134	142	150
5'6''	138	146	154
5'7''	142	150	158
5'8''	146	154	162
5'9''	150	158	166
5'10''	154	162	170
5'11''	158	166	176
6'0''	164	172	182
6'1''	170	178	188
6'2''	178	184	194
6'3''	184	190	200

[1] Adapted from various sources.
[2] To obtain barefoot height men should as a rule subtract 1'' from measured height with shoes on.

TABLE II

NORMAL WEIGHT FOR WOMEN OF SMALL, MEDIUM, AND LARGE FRAME [3]

(Weight and height as ordinarily dressed but without shoes and heavy outer clothing such as suit jackets.)

Height [4]	Small Frame	Medium Frame	Large Frame
4'9''	106	114	122
4'10''	108	116	124
4'11''	110	118	126
5'0''	113	121	129
5'1''	116	124	132
5'2''	120	128	136
5'3''	123	132	140
5'4''	127	136	144
5'5''	130	139	148
5'6''	134	142	152
5'7''	138	146	156
5'8''	142	150	160
5'9''	146	154	163
5'10''	150	158	166
5'11''	154	162	170
6'0''	158	166	174

[3] Adapted from various sources.
[4] To obtain barefoot height women should as a rule subtract 2'' from normal height with shoes on.

TABLE III
PREDICTED DAILY CALORIE NEEDS FOR WOMEN OF NORMAL WEIGHT* †[1]

Height	15-19	20-29	30-39	40-49	50-59	60-69	70-79
4'9''	2080	1890	1810	1760	1710	1480	1370
4'10''	2110	1920	1840	1790	1740	1510	1400
4'11''	2140	1950	1870	1820	1770	1530	1430
5'0''	2190	1980	1900	1850	1800	1550	1450
5'1''	2240	2020	1940	1890	1850	1590	1480
5'2''	2290	2060	1980	1950	1900	1640	1510
5'3''	2350	2100	2030	2000	1950	1690	1550
5'4''	2400	2150	2080	2040	2000	1740	1590
5'5''	2460	2200	2140	2080	2050	1780	1640
5'6''	2520	2250	2190	2120	2100	1820	1690
5'7''	2570	2300	2240	2160	2150	1860	1730
5'8''	2620	2350	2290	2220	2200	1910	1770
5'9''	2680	2400	2340	2260	2250	1950	1800
5'10''	2740	2450	2400	2310	2300	1990	1830
5'11''	2800	2500	2450	2360	2350	2040	1880
6'0''	2860	2550	2500	2410	2400	2090	1930

* If you are overweight, add 4 calories for each pound over your ideal weight as found in Table II.
† These figures are calculated from the normal basal energy requirements with an allowance for activity of 60% for the 15-19 age group, 50% for ages 20-59, and 40% for ages 60 and over. These figures apply for most overweight housewives who do their own housework, for clerical and office workers, machinery operators, domestic workers, and those in similar occupations. People engaging in heavier occupations need 10%-20% more, and people who are retired or engaged in little or no activity need about 10% less.
[1] From *Quarterly Bulletin*, Department of Health, City of New York.

TABLE IV
PREDICTED DAILY CALORIE NEEDS FOR MEN OF NORMAL WEIGHT* †[1]

Height	15-19	20-29	30-39	40-49	50-59	60-69	70-79
5'0''	2620	2250	2100	2020	1980	1710	1570
5'1''	2690	2310	2160	2070	2020	1750	1610
5'2''	2750	2390	2220	2110	2070	1790	1650
5'3''	2820	2450	2280	2160	2110	1830	1690
5'4''	2880	2500	2340	2200	2160	1880	1740
5'5''	2940	2560	2400	2260	2200	1920	1780
5'6''	3000	2620	2460	2320	2250	1950	1810
5'7''	3070	2680	2520	2380	2310	2000	1850
5'8''	3140	2740	2580	2440	2370	2060	1900
5'9''	3200	2800	2640	2500	2430	2100	1930
5'10''	3280	2880	2710	2560	2490	2160	1990
5'11''	3360	2950	2790	2620	2550	2210	2040
6'0''	3440	3030	2860	2680	2610	2250	2070
6'1''	3520	3130	2940	2740	2670	2310	2130
6'2''	3600	3180	3010	2800	2730	2370	2180
6'3''	3680	3250	3090	2860	2790	2410	2220

* If you are overweight, add 4 calories for each pound over your ideal weight as found in Table I.
† These figures are calculated from the normal basal energy requirements with an allowance for activity of 60% for the 15-19 age group, 50% for ages 20-59, and 40% for ages 60 and over. These figures apply for most overweight men who are white-collar workers, machinery operators, chauffeurs, and those in similar occupations. People engaging in heavier occupations require 10%-20% more, and people who are retired or engaged in little or no activity require about 10% less.
[1] From *Quarterly Bulletin*, Department of Health, City of New York.

COUNTDOWN ON CALORIES

1,000-CALORIE DIET PLAN FOR ADULTS
I—DIET PATTERN

Food	Household Measure	Calorie Count
Skim milk	2 cups	170
Cottage cheese	1 cup	200
Egg	1 medium	75
Selected meat, fish, or poultry	1 medium portion (6 oz.)	275 [1]
12½-calorie-count vegetables	All you want	50
Optional Calorie Budget		230
	Total	1000

II—SUGGESTED DISTRIBUTION OF OPTIONAL CALORIES

A

1 portion .... 50-calorie bread
2 portions .... 50-calorie fruits
3 portions .... 25-calorie vegetables

B

2 portions .... 25-calorie breads
1 portion .... 75-calorie fruit
1 portion .... 75-calorie fruit
2 portions .... 25-calorie vegetables

C

1 portion .... 100-calorie cereal
3 portions .... 25-calorie fruits
2 portions .... 25-calorie vegetables

III—SUGGESTED MENUS

A

Breakfast
½ cup orange juice
1 egg, soft-cooked or poached
1 thin slice bread
Beverage

Lunch
1 cup cottage cheese
Salad—lettuce, tomato,
  celery, watercress

Dinner
½ cup tomato juice
6 oz. roast veal
½ cup beets
½ cup grated carrot salad
1 pear
Beverage

Bedtime
1 cup skim milk

B

Breakfast
½ grapefruit
1 cup cottage cheese
2 pieces Melba toast
Beverage

Lunch
Salad—1 hard-cooked egg,
  celery, tomato, lettuce
1 cup skim milk

Dinner
6 oz. hamburger, broiled
½ cup beets
½ cup Brussels sprouts
Cabbage salad
1 apple
Beverage

Bedtime
1 cup skim milk

C

Breakfast
1 orange
⅔ cup oatmeal
1 cup skim milk
1 egg, soft-cooked or poached
Beverage

Lunch
Celery curls
8 oz. chicken breast [2]
1 cup carrots
1 cup skim milk
6 spears asparagus
Beverage

Dinner
6 oz. broiled flounder
Salad—escarole, endive,
  celery, green pepper
1 cup strawberries
Beverage

Bedtime
1 cup skim milk

730

[1] Meat, fish, or poultry may be chosen from the lean, medium lean, or the medium fat group. Each group must be chosen with equal frequency.

[2] 8 oz. chicken breast (200 calories) substituted for 1 cup of cottage cheese (200 calories).

1,200-CALORIE DIET PLAN FOR ADULTS

I—DIET PATTERN

Food	Household Measure	Calorie Count
Skim milk	2 cups	170
Cottage cheese	1 cup	200
Egg	1 medium	75
Selected meat, fish, or poultry	1 medium portion (6 oz.)	275 [1]
12½-calorie-count vegetables	All you want	50
Optional Calorie Budget		430
	Total	1200

II—SUGGESTED DISTRIBUTION OF OPTIONAL CALORIES

A

1 portion	50-calorie bread
2 portions	50-calorie fruits
1 portion	75-calorie fruit
2 portions	25-calorie vegetables
1 portion	75-calorie vegetable
1 portion	75-calorie egg

B

3 portions	25-calorie breads
4 portions	50-calorie fruits
2 portions	25-calorie vegetables
1 portion	100-calorie vegetable

C

1 portion	100-calorie cereal
2 portions	50-calorie fruits
1 portion	75-calorie fruit
3 portions	50-calorie vegetables

III—SUGGESTED MENUS

A

Breakfast
½ cup orange juice
2 eggs, soft-cooked or poached
1 thin slice bread
Beverage

Lunch
1 cup cottage cheese
Salad—lettuce, sliced tomato, cucumber
½ cup fruit cocktail
1 cup skim milk

Dinner
6 oz. broiled liver
½ cup peas
1 cup carrots
½ cup cabbage
1 apple
Beverage

Bedtime
1 cup skim milk

B

Breakfast
½ grapefruit
½ cup cottage cheese
1 piece Melba toast
Beverage

Lunch
4 oz. shrimp [2]
1 egg, hard-cooked
Salad—lettuce, celery, green pepper, radishes
2 pieces Melba toast
½ cup fresh pineapple
1 cup skim milk

Dinner
6 oz. broiled haddock
½ cup potato
1 cup beets
Lettuce and tomato salad
1 tangerine
Beverage

Bedtime
1 cup skim milk
1 plum

C

Breakfast
1 orange
⅔ cup corn flakes
1 egg, soft-cooked or poached
1 cup skim milk
Beverage

Lunch
4 oz. canned salmon [3]
Salad—lettuce, celery, radishes, cucumber, green peppers
3 slices tomato
1 apple
Beverage

Dinner
6 oz. roast beef
½ cup parsnips
1 cup onions
Mixed green salad
½ cup peaches
Beverage

Bedtime
1 cup skim milk

731

[1] Meat, fish, or poultry may be chosen from the lean, medium lean, or the medium fat group. Each group must be chosen with equal frequency.

[2] 4 oz. shrimp (100 calories) substituted for ½ cup cottage cheese (100 calories).

[3] 4 oz. canned salmon (170 calories) substituted for 1 cup cottage cheese (200 calories).

HOW TEENAGERS CAN STRIP OFF POUNDS
By Morton B. Glenn, M.D.

At summer camps for overweight teenagers, we have found that just about every teenager can lose weight on a sound diet. You can, too. For a weight-loss diet to be successful, it has to be nutritionally sound and satisfy your needs. Along with this, you need confidence that the diet *will* help you lose weight.

• Is it safe to diet? Yes, it is safe to diet at any age if the dieting is done correctly. A diet that does not meet nutritional needs may result in inhibition of growth—and most of you will want to reach your full growth potential. The weight-loss diets we give here are sound, fully nutritious and safe. And skin problems won't develop because of poor food choices.

• Do you need a doctor's supervision? If you are just a few pounds overweight, you probably won't need medical supervision. If you are more than 10% overweight, you should have the benefit of a medical examination and supervision of your weight-loss program. Few teenagers, however, need medication to diet successfully.

• How fast can you lose? A good diet should take off 75 pounds in a year for a teenager and over 50 pounds a year for a sub-teen. Sounds like a lot, doesn't it? It *is* a lot. Yet some simple arithmetic will show that this amounts to about 1½ pounds a week for the teenager and about one pound per week for the sub-teen.

We have seen that most weight is lost the first week; the second week, somewhat less. And the third week? Often, *none*. I call it "quitter's week." This is when weight loss may level off, and the dieter may say: "Why should I diet if I don't lose weight?" Don't let this plateau put you off. You'll lose the next week if you stay on your diet—and thereafter at a fairly steady rate. Teenage girls, by the way, may retain water and not lose weight the week before their menstrual period, but they will lose double the next week.

• How often should you weigh? Try not to weigh yourself a hundred times a day. Once a week is enough—and at the same time of day. Perhaps before breakfast, to get the most encouragement.

• How long should you stay on a diet? A diet is really worthwhile only if it accomplishes its goal permanently. Weight can be kept off permanently only if one has sound eating habits. And a weight-loss diet should simply be a refinement of correct eating habits. After dieting, when you reach a desirable weight, you drop the super-refinements and are left with the good eating habits.

• How active are you? At summer camp, we have found that overweight youngsters are usually not so physically active as normal-weight youngsters. Exercise helps your general fitness and also keeps you busy.

• Suppose you slip? Most diet repeaters tell us the same thing: They regained weight because they lapsed from their good eating habits. If you get discouraged because you have a week when you don't lose because you made a mistake or a series of mistakes, don't get discouraged. Start again with the full diet—not by eating less than the diet allows to make up for your mistakes. Once back on the diet, you will begin to lose weight again.

•How much should you weigh? Height-weight charts are a good measure of overweight. To make it easier, I have included charts that I consider best for teenagers. Judge frame by wrist size and foot width. Tiny wrists or narrow feet usually mean a small frame; very broad wrists or wide feet usually mean a large frame. Of course, most people have a medium frame.

WEIGHT CHART FOR SUB-TEENS
(Ages 10-12 in indoor clothing)

HEIGHT (with-out shoes)	BOYS Weight Pounds	GIRLS Weight Pounds
4'0''	48-58	48-58
4'1''	48-60	50-62
4'2''	52-64	53-68
4'3''	55-67	55-72
4'4''	58-70	58-74
4'5''	60-74	61-76
4'6''	63-78	64-78
4'7''	66-81	67-82
4'8''	69-85	70-86
4'9''	72-89	73-90
4'10''	76-93	76-95
4'11''	79-97	78-99
5'0''	82-101	82-104
5'1''	86-106	89-110
5'2''	90-111	94-115
5'3''	95-117	99-120

WEIGHT CHART FOR TEENAGERS
(Ages 13-19 in indoor clothing)

Height (without shoes)	BOYS Weight Pounds	GIRLS Weight Pounds
4'4''	58-72	
4'5''	61-75	64-78
4'6''	64-79	66-80
4'7''	67-81	69-86
4'8''	70-88	73-91
4'9''	74-91	76-101
4'10''	77-95	79-111
4'11''	80-99	83-115
5'0''	84-106	87-122
5'1''	87-117	91-127
5'2''	92-128	95-130
5'3''	96-140	99-132
5'4''	100-143	104-135
5'5''	104-147	108-139
5'6''	107-152	112-143
5'7''	112-156	115-148
5'8''	119-162	118-152
5'9''	123-167	122-156
5'10''	129-171	123-158
5'11''	133-176	124-159
6'0''	138-180	
6'1''	141-184	
6'2''	144-188	

(Note: The lower numbers in the range are for the younger ages and smaller frames, and the higher numbers are for the older ages and larger frames.)

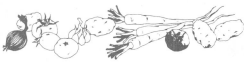

TEENAGE DIET PLAN

This diet works. Some people say it must be too much food. It is not! In order for the diet to do the most for you, *no meal may be skipped.* And remember the golden rule of dieting: *How little one eats is not so important as how correctly one eats.*

BASIC RULES

• **Choosing.** The largest calorie savings can be accomplished by paying most attention to the main course of each meal. Choose chicken, fish, shellfish and veal in place of beef and lamb as much as possible, and never use pork or pork products such as bacon or luncheon meats. When you do select beef or lamb, use lean cuts only. The best rule for meat control is never to have beef or lamb more than three lunches and three dinners per week. Fewer times would be better.

• **Preparation.** Boil, steam, poach, broil or bake. Never use fats in cooking but, when necessary, baste with lemon or tomato juice (try heating it before using it for basting) or consommé.

• **Portion control—measure carefully.** Use postage or household scales for weighing; measuring cups for liquids.

• **Variety.** Vary the fruits and vegetables and, to ensure a caloric balance as well as an adequate variety of minerals and vitamins, never use the same vegetable two days in a row.

• **Once a day.** In place of fruit and one glass of milk, you may have ½ cup (4 oz.; volume measure, not weight) of ice cream or ice milk. Yes, once a day.

• **Eat slowly,** and do any eating, no matter what, *sitting down*—never standing.

SPECIAL NO-NOs

• No grapes, cherries or watermelon (too difficult to control the amounts).
• No canned fruits unless dietetic-packed.
• No starch vegetables (potatoes, rice, corn, spaghetti, noodles, lima beans, kidney beans, chick peas).
• No salad dressings, except lemon juice, tomato juice or vinegar; no oil.
• No sugar, jams, jellies or honey.
• No butter, margarine or oil.
• No nuts, candy, potato chips, pretzels, cake or pie.

733

COUNTDOWN ON CALORIES

For each diet there is a minimum and a maximum amount of milk allowed:

Sub-teen (Boys and Girls) 8—12 years	Teenage Girls 12—18 years	Teenage Boys 12—18 years
Minimum: 2 (8-oz.) glasses Prefer: 3 Maximum: 3	Minimum: 2 (8-oz.) glasses Prefer: 2 or 3 Maximum: 3	Minimum: 2 (8-oz.) glasses Prefer: 3 Maximum: 3

All milk must be skim, and each serving is 1 cup (8-oz. glass). The other beverages allowed are water, black coffee or tea, or dietetic sodas without sugar—(less than 1 calorie per ounce).

BREAKFAST

Sub-teen (Boys and Girls)	Teenage Girls	Teenage Boys
½ cup (4 oz.) orange or grapefruit (no added sugar) or tomato juice), or 1 orange or ½ grapefruit	½ cup (4 oz.) orange or grapefruit (no added sugar) or tomato juice, or 1 orange or ½ grapefruit	½ cup (4 oz.) orange or grapefruit (no added sugar) or tomato juice, or 1 orange or ½ grapefruit
1 egg (made without fat) or ¼ cup (2 oz.) cottage cheese, or 1 slice (1 oz.) processed American cheese	1 egg (made without fat) or ¼ cup (2 oz.) cottage cheese, or 1 slice (1 oz.) processed American cheese	2 eggs (made without fat) or ½ cup (4 oz.) cottage cheese, or 1½ slices (1½ oz.) processed American cheese
1 slice of *thin-sliced* toast	1 slice of *thin-sliced* toast	1 slice of *thin-sliced* toast
Skim milk	Skim milk	Skim milk
	Coffee, tea	Coffee, tea

On all above breakfasts, in place of 1 egg and 1 slice of toast, you may have 1 "individual" package of any nonsugared cold cereal or ½ cup of hot cereal, with skim milk.

LUNCH

Lunch is best, when dieting, if eaten at home or taken to school. If a hot lunch is served at school and must be eaten, consider the school lunch as the dinner meal and have one of the following lunches at supper time.

Sub-teen (Boys and Girls)	Teenage Girls	Teenage Boys
1 sandwich using 2 slices of bread with 3 oz. of meat, fish, or poultry, or 1½ oz. processed American cheese, or 2 eggs	1 open *or* closed sandwich (1 *or* 2 slices of bread) with 3 oz. of meat, fish or poultry, or 1½ oz. of processed American cheese, or 2 eggs, or ⅔ cup (5 oz.) cottage cheese	1 or 2 full sandwiches (2 to 4 slices of bread) with up to 6 oz. meat, fish, or poultry (up to 3 oz. per sandwich) or 3 oz. of processed American cheese (up to 1½ oz. per sandwich), or 2 eggs and 1 other sandwich (as above)
May add lettuce and sliced tomato to sandwich	May add lettuce and sliced tomato to sandwich, or nibble on any raw vegetable	Instead of 1 slice bread, may substitute ½ cup of a cooked vegetable
Raw carrots, celery or any raw vegetable to nibble on	If the sandwich was open (only 1 slice bread), may have 1 fruit	May add any raw vegetables, including sliced tomato
1 fruit	Beverage	1 fruit
Beverage		Beverage

Sometimes, especially if skim milk is not available at school, lunch is a very good time to have a small cup (4 oz.) of ice cream, and give up 1 glass of milk and 1 fruit. Then you don't have to feel like an outsider and aren't tempted by your friends to cheat.

734

AFTERNOON SNACK

Almost everybody gets hungry after school. If care isn't taken here, this is the most likely time to go off a diet and eat everything from candy to pizza! This is prevented by having a definite snack of one fruit and beverage. If still hungry, lots of raw vegetables. If carrots, celery and green-pepper sticks are cleaned and cut and stored in plastic bags in the refrigerator, they will always be fresh and available, too.

DINNER

As a starter, all dinners may begin with clear soup, or ½ cup (4 oz.) of tomato, clam or diet cranberry juice.

Sub-teen (Boys and Girls)	Teenage Girls	Teenage Boys
4 to 6 oz. meat, fish, chicken. (2 thin slices meat, 2 pieces fish or 1 quarter small chicken)	4 to 6 oz. meat, fish, chicken. (2 thin slices meat, 2 pieces fish or 1 quarter small chicken)	6 to 8 oz. meat, fish, chicken. (3 thin slices meat, 3 pieces fish or ½ very small chicken)
1 or 2 portions of cooked vegetables, each ½ cup	1 or 2 portions of cooked vegetables, each ½ cup	1 or 2 portions of cooked vegetables, each ½ cup
Raw vegetable salad	Raw vegetable salad	Raw vegetable salad
1 fruit	1 fruit	1 slice bread (optional)
Skim milk	Skim milk	1 fruit
	Coffee or tea	Skim milk
		Coffee or tea

Occasionally you may substitute a portion of low-calorie fruit-flavor gelatin instead of fruit.

EVENING SNACK

(Optional) 1 fruit and beverage

EXTRAS

Sub-teen (Girls or Boys) Only

2 cookies per week; 1 starch serving (½ cup potato or ½ cup spaghetti without sauce) per week.

735

TEENAGERS' 7-DAY DIET MENUS

	Breakfast	Lunch	Dinner

Sunday	Half grapefruit
	¾ cup cold cereal
	   or
	Scrambled egg
	Toast
	Skim milk
	Coffee or tea
		*Roast Chicken
		Asparagus
		Celery, carrot sticks,
		  cucumber
		½ cup ice milk (no skim
		  milk)
		Coffee or tea
			Salad bowl
			Tuna fish (3 oz. about
			  ½ cup)
			¼ hard-cooked egg
			½ tomato
			Half banana
			Skim milk
			Coffee or tea

Monday	Half banana
	¾ cup cold cereal
	   or
	½ cup cooked whole-wheat
	  cereal
	Skim milk
	Coffee or tea
		Sectioned orange
		½ cup cottage cheese
		2 slices Melba toast
		Low-calorie fruit flavor
		  gelatin
		Skim milk
		Coffee or tea
			*Veal Patties and Mushrooms
			Carrots
			Green salad—*Zero
			  Dressing
			Pear
			Skim milk
			Coffee or tea

Tuesday	½ cup (4 oz.) orange
	  juice
	¾ cup cold cereal
	   or
	French toast
	Skim milk
	Coffee or tea
		*Sloppy Joes
		½ hamburger roll
		*Cucumber Salad
		1 tangerine
		Skim milk
		Coffee or tea
			*Napa Fish
			Green beans
			Lettuce, tomato
			Low-calorie fruit-flavor gelatin
			Skim milk
			Coffee or tea

Wednesday	½ cup (4 oz.) orange or
	  grapefruit juice
	¾ cup cold cereal
	
	   or
	Hard-cooked egg
	Toast
	Skim milk
	Coffee or tea
		Sandwich:
		Bread, 2 thin slices
		Turkey, about 2 thin slices
		  (3 oz.)
		Mustard
		Pickle
		*Baked Apple
		Low-calorie carbonated
		  beverage
			*Sweet and Sour Meat Balls
			*Napaghetti
			
			Dill pickle chips
			Fresh fruit cup
			½ cup skim milk
			Coffee or tea

Thursday	Quartered orange
	¾ cup cold cereal
	   or
	½ cup cooked farina
	Skim milk
	Coffee or tea
		*Spanish Omelet—Marinara
		Wax beans
		Tossed salad—*Zero
		  Dressing
		2 crisp rye crackers
		Apple
		Skim milk
		Coffee or tea
			2 frankfurters
			Sauerkraut
			Mustard
			1 pear
			Low-calorie carbonated beverage

Friday	½ cup (4 oz.) grapefruit juice ¾ cup cold cereal or *Cinnamon "Danish" Skim milk Coffee or tea	½ cup (4 oz.) tomato juice *Napa Cheese Puffs Celery—carrot sticks Cucumbers ½ cup canned pineapples Skim milk Coffee or tea	Roast Beef (4"x3"x1") Broccoli Pickled beets Ice milk (no skim milk) Coffee or tea
Saturday	½ cup (4 oz.) orange juice ¾ cup cold cereal or *Cheese Toast Skim milk Coffee or tea	Hamburger (3 oz.) ½ hamburger roll Sliced onion Lettuce, tomato Apple Skim milk Coffee or tea	*Chicken Cacciatore Spinach Green salad—*Zero Dressing ½ cup canned pineapple Skim milk Coffee or tea

*Recipes for starred dishes on following page. Menus and recipes adapted from Camp Naponoch Menu Plan, Ellenville, N.Y.

TEENAGERS' DIET RECIPES

Roast Chicken
Makes 4 servings

Place 2½ lb. chicken, quartered, in a baking pan. Sprinkle with salt, pepper, monosodium glutamate, paprika. Roast in 400° oven until brown—about 45 minutes.

Veal Patties and Mushrooms
Makes 4 servings

1 Buy 1½ lbs. unbreaded veal patties or make your own. Season with salt, pepper and mono-sodium glutamate.
2 Combine ½ cup beef bouillon, ½ cup tomato juice and pour over patties.
3 Let stand 15-20 minutes.
4 Add 1 can (3 to 4 oz.) sliced mushrooms.
5 Bake in oven at 400°, 20-25 minutes.
6 Drain liquid and serve as sauce.
7 Just before serving, place patties under broiler, 4-5 minutes.

Zero Dressing
Makes ¾ cup (Recipe can be doubled)

½ cup tomato juice
2 tablespoons lemon juice
1 teaspoon salt
1 teaspoon grated onion
1 clove garlic, minced
½ teaspoon prepared mustard
½ teaspoon Worcestershire sauce
granulated or liquid no-calorie sweetner

Shake all ingredients in a jar with a screw top, using your favorite no-calorie sweetener to taste. Store in refrigerator. Shake again before serving.

Sloppy Joes
Makes 6 cups

2½ pounds ground lean beef
2 to 3 chopped onions (2-3 cups)
Salt and pepper
Sauce
1 can (6 ounce) tomato paste
½ cup (4 ounce) catsup
¼ cup (2 ounce) tomato juice
2 tablespoons Worcestershire sauce
2 tablespoons prepared mustard
2 tablespoons lemon juice
Granulated or liquid no-calorie sweetner

1 Cook beef and onion together, seasoning to taste with salt and pepper, until done. Stir often. Drain off all liquid and fat from pan.
2 Make sauce: Combine all sauce ingredients in a saucepan, using your favorite no-calorie sweetener to taste.
3 Cook, stirring often to prevent sticking, 15-20 minutes, or until very thick. Pour over meat and keep hot until serving time. Use ¼ cup (2 ounce) serving for lunch, ½ cup (4 ounce) serving for dinner. Serve on ½ hamburger roll. (Left over can be frozen. This recipe can be cut in half.)

Cucumber Salad
Makes 4 servings

Slice 4 cucumbers very thin. Place in bowl with 1 teaspoon salt. Cover with water and chill overnight. Pour off liquid and add 1 cup vinegar and your favorite granulated or liquid sweetener to taste. Sliced onions can be added.

Napa Fish
Makes 2 servings

1 Use flounder or haddock filet. Divide 1 pound fish into two serving portions (about 8 oz. each). Place in shallow baking dish and season with salt, pepper and monosodium glutamate. Add 2 tablespoons lemon juice and 2 tablespoons tomato juice. Marinate about 1½ to 2 hours.
2 Bake fish with marinade in 350° oven about 20-25 minutes. Remove from oven. Drain off liquid and serve as sauce. Add ½ cup (2 ounces) grated American cheese. Place under broiler for 3-4 minutes or until cheese melts and begins to brown.

Baked Apple
Makes 1 serving

Core and peel ½-inch of skin from top of 1 apple. Turn top side down in small baking dish. Pour ½ cup cherry-flavored low-calorie carbonated beverage over. Bake in 350° oven for 45 minutes.

737

COUNTDOWN ON CALORIES

Sweet-and-Sour Meat Balls
Makes 4 servings

Combine 1 pound ground lean veal or beef with salt and pepper and monosodium glutamate, if desired. Shape into meat balls. Combine 1 cup tomato juice, 1 cup water, 1 teaspoon instant beef broth, 1 teaspoon lemon juice and your favorite no-calorie sweetener to taste in a saucepan. Add meat balls and simmer 1 hour. Good served over NAPAGHETTI (recipe follows).

Napaghetti
Makes 4 servings

Drain 1 can (1 pound, 13 ounces) bean sprouts and place in saucepan. Cover with cold water. Cook for 20 minutes, until soft. Drain; pour sauce over. Sprinkle *lightly* with Parmesan cheese, if desired.

Sauce

1½ cups (12 ounces) tomato juice
 2 teaspoons onion flakes
 1 clove garlic, crushed
   Salt and pepper
   Liquid no-calorie sweetener

Combine ingredients, using your favorite no-calorie sweetener to taste, in a saucepan. Cook until thick.

Spanish Omelet
Makes 1 serving

Beat 2 eggs together. Add salt, pepper, and brown 1 side in nonstick pan (no fat); flip over. Cover half of omelet with ¼ cup MARINARA SAUCE (recipe follows). Fold over and serve.

738

Marinara Sauce
Makes 6 cups

 1 can (46 ounces) tomato juice
 2 green peppers, halved, seeded and chopped
 1 red pepper, halved, seeded, and chopped
 2 teaspoons chopped onion
 ½ teaspoon leaf basil, crumbled
   Dash of garlic powder
 1 can (3 to 4 ounces) sliced mushrooms
 ½ teaspoon leaf oregano, crumbled

Combine all ingredients, except mushrooms and oregano in a saucepan. Cook, uncovered, for 35 minutes. Add mushrooms and oregano and cook 10 minutes longer. Add 1 envelope (1 teaspoon) instant beef broth, if desired. Use ¼ cup for each serving.

Cinnamon "Danish"
Makes 1 serving

 1 slice thin white bread, toasted
 ¼ cup (2 ounces) cottage cheese
   Liquid no-calorie sweetener
   Cinnamon

Shake a few drops liquid no-calorie sweetener on top of cheese, spread on bread, sprinkle with cinnamon. Put under broiler until hot and bubbly.

Napa Cheese Puffs
Makes 1 serving

 1 slice thin white bread
 2 slices (2 ounces) processed American cheese, shredded
 2 tablespoons tomato juice
   Dash of oregano and garlic powder

Combine cheese, tomato juice, oregano and garlic. Spread evenly on bread. Broil until cheese melts.

Cheese Toast
Makes 1 serving

 1 slice thin white bread
 1 slice (1 ounce) processed American cheese

Place cheese on bread; broil until cheese is melted.

Chicken Cacciatore
Makes 4 servings

Place 1 broiler-fryer, (about 2½ pounds), cut up, in shallow baking dish. Sprinkle with salt, pepper, monosodium glutamate, garlic powder. Cut 1 small green pepper into rings; thinly slice 1 onion; arrange on top of chicken and pour 1 can (1 lb.) tomatoes over. Roast in 350° oven until done, about 45–50 minutes.

31 DINNERS UNDER 500 CALORIES

1

6 cherrystone clams with lemon wedges
¼ broiled chicken
6 spears cooked asparagus with 1 teaspoon regular butter or margarine
½ cup steamed yellow squash
*Cabbage Relish Salad
1 tangerine
1 vanilla wafer
1 cup skim milk
Black coffee or tea with lemon

2

¾ cup condensed onion soup, diluted
*Bavarian Pork and Kraut
½ cup cooked peas and carrots
1 cup bite-size salad greens with 1 tablespoon low-calorie Russian dressing
*Lemon-Lime Sparkle
Black coffee or tea with lemon

3

1 veal chop (6 ounces) braised in bouillon
6 broiled mushrooms caps
½ cup steamed green beans
3 raw cauliflowerets, 6 carrot sticks, and ½ small tomato on lettuce
1 thin slice French bread
*Blushing Pear Square
Black coffee or tea with lemon

4

¾ cup jellied consommé
1 slice lean baked ham (4 inches square, ¼ inch thick)
½ medium sweet potato, baked
½ cup steamed spinach seasoned with vinegar
*Lettuce Slices with Radish Cream Dressing
*Pineapple Puff
Black coffee or tea with lemon

5

Shrimp cocktail (15 tiny shrimps, 1 tablespoon chili sauce)
1 slice broiled liver (3 inches square, ¼ inch thick)
1 medium tomato, broiled
½ cup plain cooked succotash
6 slices cucumber and ½ cup chicory with 1 tablespoon low-calorie French dressing
*Molded Cheese Snow with Strawberries
Black coffee or tea with lemon

6

Broiled cheeseburger on ½ hamburger bun (4 ounces lean ground round and 1 tablespoon grated Cheddar cheese)
1 cup steamed cauliflowerets
1 small tomato, stewed
8 each celery and green-pepper sticks with seasoned salt
½ glass skim milk
2 diet-pack peach halves
Black coffee or tea with lemon

7

¾ cup chicken with rice soup
2 square saltines
3 small broiled lobster tails with 1 tablespoon low-calorie margarine
1 cup Brussels sprouts with vinegar
*Double Bean Salad Bowl
*Chocolate-Almond Roll
½ cup skim milk
Black coffee or tea with lemon

8

1 cup mixed vegetable juice
2½ slices canned corned beef (¼ inch thick)
1 small boiled potato with parsley
1 cup steamed cabbage
*Pimiento-Petal Salad
½ cup diced fresh pineapple with mint
1 small chocolate wafer
Black coffee or tea with lemon

9

¾ cup madriléne
*Lamb and Vegetables en Brochette
1 cup bite-size iceberg lettuce, ½ cup cooked julienne carrots, and ¼ cup sliced celery with 1 tablespoon low-calorie French dressing
*Double Orange Coupe
Black coffee or tea with lemon

10

*Pot-au-Feu with Bonus Broth
1 cup bite-size salad greens and ⅓ cup sliced fresh strawberries with 1 tablespoon low-calorie mayonnaise
½ cup low-calorie lemon gelatin
Black coffee or tea with lemon

11

1 cup beef bouillon
1 piece broiled swordfish (3 inches square, ½ inch thick)
⅓ cup cooked lima beans
1 cup steamed yellow squash
½ cup chilled artichoke hearts with 1 tablespoon low-calorie Italian dressing
*French Fruit Pie
Black coffee or tea with lemon

12

*Meat Balls Scandia
⅔ cup cooked noodles
6 spears cooked asparagus and 1 cup bite-size chicory with 1 tablespoon low-calorie Thousand Island dressing
2 diet-pack pear halves
2 small sugar wafers
Black coffee or tea with lemon

13

*Watercress Cream
1 small chicken breast, fried
1 small baked potato with seasoned salt
1 cup cooked zucchini slices marinated in 1 tablespoon low-calorie French dressing on lettuce
½ cup fresh whole strawberries with no-calorie sweetener
Black coffee or tea with lemon

14
1 broiled ground-round patty (4 ounces)
½ cup steamed sliced onions
½ cup green peas
½ cup pickled beets on lettuce
*Glazed Fruit Meringues
½ glass skim milk
Black coffee or tea with lemon

15
2 slices roast turkey breast (3 inches
square, ¼ inch thick)
1 cup riced potato and carrot
1 cup steamed Brussels sprouts with lemon juice
1 small tomato filled with ½ cup cooked wax beans
on lettuce with 1 tablespoon low-calorie
Italian dressing
½ cup diet-pack apricot halves
Black coffee or tea with lemon

16
*Clam Dip Appeteaser
2 thin lean pork chops braised in bouillon
1 cup steamed Chinese cabbage
2 cooked large whole carrots with mint
1 seasoned-rye wafer
½ cup unsweetened applesauce
Black coffee or tea with lemon

17
½ cup unsweetened melon balls
4 chicken livers, 1 slice bacon, and 3 small onions
brushed with Worcestershire sauce,
all broiled on skewer
*Saucepan Risotto
*Cabbage Relish Salad
½ cup low-calorie butterscotch pudding
Black coffee or tea with lemon

18
1 broiled loin lamb chop (6 ounces)
1 cup chopped broccoli cooked in bouillon
½ cup mashed yellow turnips
1 cup shredded lettuce and 4 sliced small radishes
with 1 tablespoon low-calorie mayonnaise
1 slice white bread
½ pat regular butter or margarine
½ cup diet-pack fruit cocktail
Black coffee or tea with lemon

19
¾ cup beef broth
*Shrimps Creole with Noodles
1 medium steamed artichoke with 1 tablespoon
low-calorie margarine
1 small head Bibb lettuce with 3 cherry tomatoes and
2 teaspoons low-calorie blue-cheese dressing
¾ cup lime water ice
Black coffee or tea with lemon

20
½ cup vegetable beef soup
1 slice roast lamb (4 inches square, ¼ inch thick)
½ medium potato, baked
*Lemon Broccoli
½ cup skim milk
½ cup fresh orange sections with mint
Black coffee or tea with lemon

21
*Oriental Chicken and Vegetables with Rice
*Pimiento-Petal Salad
1 small cloverleaf roll
½ pat regular butter or margarine
½ cup diet-pack mandarin-orange segments
Black coffee or tea with lemon

22
*Egg Salad en Gelée
*Veal Fricassee
1 cup mixed green beans and diced carrots, steamed
½ cup vanilla ice milk
Black coffee or tea with lemon

23
½ cup diet-pack grapefruit sections
1 piece poached salmon (3 inches square,
½ inch thick)
6 spears steamed asparagus with 1 teaspoon low-
calorie margarine
½ cup mashed potato (with milk only)
*Two-Tomato Salad Molds
½ cup plain skim-milk yogurt
Black coffee or tea with lemon

24
1 cup low-calorie cranberry-juice cocktail
1 slice sirloin or eye-round beef roast (4 inches square,
¼ inch thick)
½ cup whole-kernel corn
1 cup shredded cabbage and 2 tablespoons diced
green pepper with 1 tablespoon low-calorie
mayonnaise
½ cup low-calorie strawberry gelatin with 1 tablespoon
low-calorie whipped topping
½ glass skim milk
Black coffee or tea with lemon

25
½ cup vegetable soup
1 slice roast veal (3 inches square, ¼ inch thick)
½ medium sweet potato, mashed
1 stalk braised Belgian endive with lemon
1 cup bite-size lettuce and 3 sliced fresh mushrooms
with 1 tablespoon low-calorie French dressing
1 small apple with 1 tablespoon uncreamed cottage
cheese and 1 square saltine
Black coffee or tea with lemon

26
½ cup orange sections in no-calorie ginger ale
*Saucy Sole Roulade
⅔ cup cooked hominy grits
¾ cup cooked diced carrots
*Asparagus Mimosa Salad
1 cup skim milk
½ cup low-calorie chocolate pudding
Black coffee or tea with lemon

27
3 slices broiled flank steak (5 inches long, ¼ inch thick)
1 small potato, baked
4 spears steamed broccoli
1 medium orange, sliced, on lettuce with 1 tablespoon
low-calorie French dressing
½ cup skim milk
1 large vanilla wafer
Black coffee or tea with lemon

28
½ cup crabmeat creamed with ½ cup skim milk and
1 tablespoon flour on ½ cup steamed rice
1 cup steamed green beans and
mushrooms with lemon wedge
2 green onions
2 medium green olives
*Pineapple Puff
Black coffee or tea with lemon

29
1 cup instant chicken broth
1 slice prime-rib roast (4 inches square, ¼ inch thick)
1 diet-pack pineapple slice with mint
½ medium sweet potato, baked
½ cup steamed kale
4 carrot curls, 1 whole canned pimiento, 6 celery sticks,
and 1 ripe olive, all in lettuce cup
*Glazed Fruit Meringues
Black coffee or tea with lemon

30
*Clam Dip Appeteaser
2 thin frankfurters
½ cup cooked sauerkraut
½ cup mashed potato (with milk only)
½ cup steamed French-style green beans
with seasoned salt
½ slice cracked wheat bread
½ pat regular butter or margarine
½ cup low-calorie cherry gelatin, whipped
Black coffee or tea with lemon

31
1 cup mixed vegetable juice
2 slices roast pork (3 inches square, ½ inch thick)
½ cup unsweetened applesauce with cinnamon
1 cup steamed Italian green beans with ½ teaspoon
sesame seeds
½ cup mushroom caps and ¼ cup sliced cooked
carrots marinated in vinegar, no-calorie sweetener,
and dillweed
½ cup low-calorie vanilla pudding with
1 diet-pack peach half
Black coffee or tea with lemon

For starred (*) recipes, see pages that follow.

WEIGHTLESS DINNERS
450 CALORIES OR FEWER

Beef-Chicken Dinner
*Pot-au-Feu with Bonus Broth
*Two-Tomato Salad Molds

Pot-au-Feu with Bonus Broth
Dieter's feast of pot roast, white meat of chicken, three vegetables, even savory broth to sip as a starter.
Makes 6 servings, 388 calories each

1 lean boneless bottom round beef roast,
   weighing about 2 pounds
8 cups water
1 large onion, chopped (1 cup)
2 cloves of garlic
2 envelopes instant beef broth
   OR: 2 beef-flavor bouillon cubes
3 teaspoons salt
6 sprigs parsley
1 bay leaf
6 peppercorns
¼ teaspoon leaf thyme, crumbled
2 whole chicken breasts, weighing about 12
   ounces each
1 package (1 pound) carrots
1 pound green beans
1 bunch leeks

1 Trim all fat from roast; place roast in a kettle. Add water, onion, garlic, beef broth or bouillon cubes, and salt. Tie parsley, bay leaf, peppercorns, and thyme in a small cheesecloth bag; add to kettle.
2 Heat to boiling; cover. Simmer 2 hours. Add chicken breasts; simmer 30 minutes longer, or until beef and chicken are tender. Remove meats to a platter; keep warm.
3 While meats cook, pare carrots and slice thin diagonally. Wash green beans and tip. Trim root ends and leafy tops from leeks; wash well in warm salted water.
4 Reheat broth in kettle to boiling; add carrots and green beans, keeping each in a separate pile; cover. Cook 15 minutes; add leeks. Cook 15 minutes longer, or until all vegetables are tender. Remove from broth with a slotted spoon; keep warm.
5 Strain broth into a large bowl, pressing onion and garlic through sieve into liquid; let stand a minute, or until fat rises to top, then skim off. Return broth to kettle; heat to boiling; cook rapidly until broth is reduced to 6 cups. Pour into soup cups or small bowls; garnish each with two or three small white onion rings, if you wish. Serve as appetizer course.
6 Carve beef and chicken into ¼-inch-thick

slices; place on heated serving plates. Split leeks lengthwise; arrange with carrots and green beans in separate piles around meats.
Weight-watcher's serving: 1 cup broth, 2 slices each beef and chicken, and 1/6 of the carrots, leeks, and green beans.

Two-Tomato Salad Molds

Shimmering molded version of gazpacho set in a circle of tomato wedges and crisp cucumber slices.
Makes 6 servings, 47 calories each

1 envelope unflavored gelatin
2 cups mixed vegetable juice
2 whole cloves
2 whole allspice
1 tablespoon lemon juice
1 small cucumber
1 cup shredded cabbage
¾ cup chopped celery
3 small tomatoes
1 tablespoon low-calorie mayonnaise

1 Soften gelatin in ½ cup of the vegetable juice in a medium-size bowl.
2 Combine remaining vegetable juice, cloves, allspice, and lemon juice in a small saucepan; heat to boiling; simmer 5 minutes. Strain over gelatin mixture in bowl, then stir until gelatin dissolves. Chill 30 minutes, or until mixture is as thick as unbeaten egg white.
3 Cut off ¼ of the cucumber; pare; chop coarsely. Fold into gelatin mixture with cabbage and celery. Spoon into 6 individual molds or custard cups. Chill several hours, or until set.
4 Score remaining unpared cucumber with a fork; slice thin. Cut tomatoes into thin wedges.
5 When ready to serve, run a small knife around tops of salads, then dip molds, one at a time, *very quickly* in and out of a pan of hot water; invert onto centers of 6 salad plates; lift off molds. Arrange cucumber slices, dividing evenly, in rings around salads; top with an overlapping ring of tomato wedges. Spoon mayonnaise on each mold; tuck parsley around bases of molds, if you wish.
Weight-watcher's serving: 1 salad mold, plus cucumber and tomato garnish and ½ teaspoon mayonnaise.

●

Old Country Pork Chop Bake
*Bavarian Pork and Kraut with Parslied Potatoes
*Egg Salads en Gelée
Rye Bread (1 small slice per serving)

Bavarian Pork and Kraut

Today's lean pork slips as sensibly into diet meals as any other meat. This time it's chops on caraway-seasoned kraut.
Bake at 350° for 1 hour. Makes 6 servings, 319 calories each

6 loin pork chops, cut 1 inch thick (about 2 pounds)
2 packages (1 pound each) sauerkraut (from meat or dairy case)
1 teaspoon caraway seeds
2 medium-size tart apples, quartered, cored, and sliced thin
1 can (12 ounces) beer
6 small potatoes, pared
2 tablespoons chopped parsley

1 Trim all fat from chops. Brown chops slowly in a medium-size frying pan.
2 Empty sauerkraut into a strainer; rinse under cold water; drain well. Combine with caraway seeds in an 8-cup baking dish. Place apple slices in a layer over sauerkraut; top with browned chops.
3 Pour off any fat from frying pan; stir in beer. Heat slowly, scraping brown bits from bottom of pan, to boiling; pour over chops; cover dish.
4 Bake in moderate oven (350°) 1 hour, or until chops are tender.
5 While meat bakes, cook potatoes in boiling salted water in a medium-size saucepan 20 minutes, or until tender; drain well.
6 Place chops, sauerkraut, and potatoes on 6 heated serving plates; sprinkle potatoes with parsley.
Weight-watcher's serving: 1 pork chop, ⅔ cup sauerkraut, and 1 potato.

Egg Salads en Gelée

Deviled egg rings on jellied beef broth. Servings are ample, so these can be salad and appetizer if you wish.
Makes 6 servings, 56 calories each

1 envelope unflavored gelatin
1 can (10½ ounces) condensed beef broth
2 hard-cooked eggs, shelled
2 tablespoons low-calorie mayonnaise
   Dash of salt
½ medium-size head iceberg lettuce
   Paprika
   Parsley

1 Soften gelatin in beef broth in a small saucepan. Heat slowly, stirring constantly, until gelatin

742

dissolves; pour into a shallow pan, 8x8x2. Chill several hours, or until set. (Tip: To speed setting, place pan of gelatin in another pan of ice and water.)

2 Cut eggs crosswise into thin slices; carefully remove yolks and place in a small bowl. Set aside 18 of the prettiest white rings, then add remainder to egg yolks; mash well with a fork. Blend in mayonnaise and salt.

3 Shred lettuce coarsely; divide evenly among 6 salad plates. Cut gelatin mixture into tiny cubes or press through a sieve into a small bowl; spoon over lettuce. Place 3 egg-white rings on top of gelatin on each plate; spoon egg-yolk mixture into centers. Sprinkle filled egg rings with paprika and garnish plates with parsley. *Weight-watcher's serving: ½ cup shredded lettuce, about ¼ cup gelatin, and 3 filled egg rings.*

Kettle Veal
*Clam Dip Appeteaser
*Veal Fricassee
*Lemon Broccoli

Clam Dip Appeteaser

Dip with plenty of snap, served with three raw vegetables. Uncreamed cottage cheese gives it its start.

Makes 6 servings, 83 calories each

  1 can (about 8 ounces) minced clams
  1 container (12 ounces) pot cheese
 ¼ cup skim milk
 ½ teaspoon onion salt
  1 teaspoon Worcestershire sauce
  6 ten-inch-long stalks of celery
  6 large cauliflowerets
  1 large stalk Belgian endive

1 Drain liquid from clams into an electric-blender container; add cheese, milk, onion salt, and Worcestershire sauce; cover. Beat several minutes, or until smooth; spoon into a medium-size bowl. (If you do not have a blender, beat same ingredients on high speed of electric mixer until smooth.)

2 Fold clams into cheese mixture; chill at least an hour to season.

3 Split celery stalks lengthwise; cut each stick into 2-inch lengths. Slice cauliflowerets thin; cut endive lengthwise into sixths.

4 When ready to serve, arrange vegetables in separate piles around edges of 6 salad plates; spoon clam mixture in centers, dividing evenly. Sprinkle clam mixture with paprika, if you wish. *Weight-watcher's serving: ¼ cup clam dip, 12 celery sticks, 1 cauliflaweret, and 1/6 stalk endive.*

French classic with its calories pruned: Pot au Feu.

Veal Fricassee

This creamy gravy won't put on pounds! It's made by stirring evaporated milk into an herb-seasoned broth.

Makes 6 servings, 265 calories each

  2 pounds lean boneless veal shoulder
  3 bay leaves
  2 teaspoons celery salt
  1 teaspoon leaf rosemary, crumbled
 ½ teaspoon pepper
  1 envelope instant beef broth
    OR: 1 beef-flavor bouillon cube
  2 cups water
1½ pounds small white onions
 ½ pound fresh mushrooms
 ¼ cup evaporated skim milk
  2 tablespoons chopped parsley

1 Trim any fat from veal; cut veal into 1-inch cubes.

2 Combine bay leaves, celery salt, rosemary, pepper, beef broth or bouillon cube, and water in a kettle or Dutch oven; add veal cubes. Heat to boiling; cover. Simmer 1 hour.

3 While veal cooks, peel onions; place on top of meat; cover. Simmer 45 minutes, or until veal and onions are tender.

4 Wash mushrooms and trim. Stir evaporated milk, then mushrooms into meat mixture; simmer 10 minutes longer. Remove bay leaves.

5 Spoon onto heated serving plates; sprinkle with parsley.
Weight-watcher's serving: 1 cupful.

743

COUNTDOWN ON CALORIES

Lemon Broccoli

Your figure can afford the generous dressing on this broccoli—it's low-calorie margarine
Makes 6 servings, 86 calories each

1 bunch broccoli (about 2 pounds)
6 tablespoons low-calorie margarine
1 tablespoon lemon juice

1 Trim outer layers and tough ends of broccoli; split any thick stalks, then cut stalks and flowerets into about-3-inch lengths.
2 Cook, covered, in boiling salted water in a medium-size saucepan 12 minutes, or just until crisply tender; drain well; return to pan.
3 Add margarine, then sprinkle with lemon juice; heat just until margarine melts. Spoon onto heated serving plates; drizzle any sauce from pan over top.
Weight-watcher's serving: 6 pieces of broccoli and about 1 tablespoon sauce.

Springtime Shrimp
Watercress Cream
Saltines (2 square crackers per serving)
Shrimps Creole with Noodles
Asparagus Mimosa Salad

Watercress Cream

Best served piping hot, this tangy soup is an amazing appetite-quencher. Your quota is a whole cupful.
Makes 6 servings, 105 calories each

2 bunches watercress
2 tablespoons flour
6 cups skim milk
2 teaspoons instant minced onion
2 teaspoons salt

1 Wash watercress and dry on paper toweling. Set aside 6 sprigs for garnish; chop remaining stems and leaves fine. (There should be about 3 cups.)
2 Smooth flour and about 4 tablespoons of the milk to a paste in a large saucepan; slowly stir in remaining milk, onion, and salt. Cook, stirring constantly, until mixture thickens slightly and boils 1 minute. Remove from heat.
3 Stir in chopped watercress. (If you prefer a smooth soup, twirl mixture, part at a time, in an electric blender.)
4 Ladle soup into heated soup plates; float a sprig of watercress on each serving. Serve hot.
Weight-watcher's serving: About 1 cup.

Shrimps Creole

Sauce is tomato-rich and brimming with shrimps, but very economical where calories are concerned.
Makes 6 servings, 226 calories each

3 medium-size onions, peeled and sliced thin
½ cup chopped green pepper
1 can (3 or 4 ounces) chopped mushrooms
½ teaspoon salt
¼ teaspoon paprika
¼ teaspoon curry powder
⅛ teaspoon pepper
1 can (about 1 pound) stewed tomatoes
   Granulated, liquid, or tablet no-calorie sweetener
3 cans (5 ounces each) deveined shrimps, drained and rinsed
3 cups hot cooked fine noodles

1 Combine onions, green pepper, mushrooms and liquid, salt, paprika, curry powder, pepper, and tomatoes in a large frying pan; stir in your favorite no-calorie sweetener, using the equivalent of 2 teaspoons sugar. Heat slowly, stirring, constantly, to boiling; simmer 10 minutes, or until onion and green pepper are tender.
2 Stir in shrimps. Simmer 10 minutes longer, or until shrimps are heated through.
3 Spoon noodles onto 6 heated serving plates; spoon shrimp mixture on top.
Weight-watcher's serving: 1 cup shrimp mixture and ½ cup noodles.

Asparagus Mimosa Salad

Salad in spring shades: Frozen asparagus seasoned in a vinegar-chive dressing with sunny sieved egg on top.
Makes 6 servings, 37 calories each

2 packages (10 ounces each) frozen asparagus spears

A beneficial weightlessness featuring Fish Française, Artichokes Parisienne and Pimiento-Petal Salads.

¼ cup cider vinegar
2 tablespoons water
1 clove of garlic, minced
¼ teaspoon salt
⅛ teaspoon paprika
1 tablespoon finely cut chives
   Granulated or liquid no-calorie sweetener
6 large lettuce leaves
1 hard-cooked egg, shelled

1 Cook asparagus, following label directions; place in a shallow dish.
2 In a cup, mix vinegar, water, garlic, salt, paprika, chives, and your favorite no-calorie sweetener, using the equivalent of 2 tablespoons sugar. Pour over asparagus. Chill at least an hour to season.
3 When ready to serve, place lettuce leaves on 6 salad plates; arrange asparagus, dividing evenly, on top. Spoon any dressing from dish over asparagus. Press egg through a sieve into a small bowl; sprinkle over asparagus.
Weight-watcher's serving: 8 asparagus spears and 1/6 of the sieved egg.

WEIGHTLESS MEALS
350 CALORIES OR FEWER

Fish Française
Grapefuit Halves (1 per serving)
*Saucy Sole Roulade
*Artichokes Parisienne
*Pimiento-Petal Salads

Pimiento-Petal Salads
Blue cheese dressing is an inspired top choice for pungent *watercress* and brilliant pimiento blossoms.
Makes 6 servings, 33 calories each

2 small heads Boston lettuce
1 bunch water cress
1 can (4 ounces) pimientos, drained
6 tablespoons low-calorie blue-cheese salad
   dressing

1 Separate lettuce leaves; trim any long or

745

coarse stems from watercress. Wash greens and dry well. Break lettuce into bite-size pieces; place on 6 salad plates; tuck water cress sprigs between pieces.

2 Dice half of the pimientos; spoon over greens. Cut remaining pimientos into 6 long strips; roll up each, jelly-roll fashion; tuck one into top of each salad. Drizzle salad dressing over all.
Weight-watcher's serving: 1 salad plate with 1 tablespoon dressing.

Artichokes Parisienne
Spring standout among vegetables looks extra sumptuous stuffed with peas, but is actually quite a calorie bargain.
Makes 6 servings, 130 calories each

6 medium-size artichokes
2 slices lemon
1 teaspoon leaf oregano, crumbled
1 teaspoon salt
⅛ teaspoon pepper
1 tablespoon vegetable oil
1 package (10 ounces) frozen green peas
1 teaspoon leaf basil, crumbled
3 tablespoons low-calorie margarine, melted

1 Wash artichokes; trim stems close to base. With a sharp knife, slice an inch off the top and snip off any spiny leaf tips.
2 Stand artichokes in a deep saucepan; add lemon, oregano, ½ teaspoon of the salt, and pepper. Drizzle ½ teaspoonful of the oil into each artichoke; pour enough water into pan to make a 2-inch depth. Heat to boiling; cover. Cook 40 minutes, or until a leaf pulls away easily from the base; drain well. Cool slightly.
3 While artichokes cook, cook peas with basil and remaining ½ teaspoon salt, following label directions; drain. Keep hot.
4 Start at center of each artichoke and, working carefully, spread leaves of each open and cut out the fuzzy choke at bottom. Place artichokes on heated serving plates; spoon peas into hollowed-out centers; drizzle melted margarine over peas and artichokes.
Weight-watcher's serving: 1 artichoke, about ¼ cup peas, and ½ tablespoon margarine.

746

Saucy Sole Roulade
Sea foods are famous for being high in protein and low in calories. Sole and crab do the honors here.

Bake at 325° for 30 minutes. Makes 6 servings, 132 calories each

1 can (about 7 ounces) crab meat, drained
½ teaspoon dry mustard
¼ teaspoon leaf marjoram, crumbled
¼ teaspoon Worcestershire sauce
6 fresh fillets of sole (about 1½ pounds)
6 peppercorns
4 bay leaves
1 teaspoon salt
1 tablespoon lemon juice
1 cup water
1 tablespoon flour
1 tablespoon catsup
1 teaspoon non-dairy coffee "cream" powder

1 Break crab meat into small chunks, removing bony tissue, if any. Place in a small bowl; mix in mustard, marjoram, and Worcestershire sauce.
2 Cut fish fillets in half lengthwise. Spoon 2 teaspoonfuls crab mixture on wide end of each piece; roll up, jelly-roll fashion; fasten with wooden picks. Stand rolls on end in a large baking dish.
3 Add peppercorns, bay leaves, salt, lemon juice, and water to baking dish; cover.
4 Bake in slow oven (325°) 30 minutes, or until fish flakes easily. Lift fish rolls carefully from liquid with a pancake turner to a platter; keep hot while making sauce.
5 Strain liquid from fish into a bowl, then measure 1 cupful into a small saucepan; discard remainder. Stir flour, catsup, and powdered "cream" into saucepan; cook, stirring constantly, until sauce thickens slightly and boils 1 minute.
6 Place fish rolls on each of 6 heated serving plates; spoon about 1 tablespoonful sauce over each. Garnish each plate with a cucumber bouquet, if you wish. (To make each, cut a 1½-inch-long chunk from a small cucumber; stand upright. Make a deep slit across top and a diagonal cut in each side. Insert a lemon wedge in top slit and a radish slice in the diagonal cuts on each side.)
Weight-watcher's serving: 2 fish rolls and 2 tablespoons sauce.

Lamb Dinner, Skewer-Style
*Lamb and Vegetables en Brochette
*Saucepan Risotto
*Lettuce Slices with Radish Cream Dressing

Lamb and Vegetables En Brochette
Lamb cubes, zucchini, and green peppers sparked with Italian dressing and served on broth-simmered rice.
Makes 6 servings, 315 calories each

> 1 shank end leg of lamb, weighing about 3½ pounds
> ¼ cup water
> ¼ cup bottled low-calorie Italian salad dressing
> 3 medium-size zucchini
> 2 medium-size green peppers
> 6 cherry tomatoes
>   SAUCEPAN RISOTTO (recipe follows)

1 Cut lamb from bone; trim off any fat, then cut meat in 1½-inch cubes. Place in a large shallow dish.
2 Mix water and Italian dressing in a cup; pour over lamb; turn pieces to coat evenly. Let stand, turning several times, 1 hour, to season.
3 While meat seasons, trim ends from zucchini, then cut each into ¼-inch-thick slices. Cut stems from green peppers, then halve lengthwise; cut out seeds and membrane. Cut each half into 3 strips. Thread zucchini and pepper pieces onto 6 small skewers. (Thread zucchini through rind so it won't slip.)
4 When meat is ready to cook, lift cubes from marinade; thread, dividing evenly, onto 6 more small skewers. Place on rack in broiler pan; brush with part of remaining marinade from dish.
5 Broil, 4 to 6 inches from heat, 6 minutes; turn. Place vegetable skewers on broiler pan; brush vegetables and lamb with marinade. Continue broiling, turning several times and brushing with more marinade, 6 to 8 minutes, or until lamb and vegetables are tender. Thread a cherry tomato on end of each vegetable skewer.
6 Spoon SAUCEPAN RISOTTO onto 6 heated serving plates; arrange lamb and vegetable skewers on top.
    SAUCEPAN RISOTTO—Combine ½ cup uncooked rice and 1 envelope instant chicken broth or 1 chicken-bouillon cube in a medium-size saucepan; stir in 1½ cups boiling water; cover. Simmer 25 minutes, or until rice is tender and liquid is absorbed. Fluff rice with a fork before serving.
Weight-watcher's serving: 1 skewer of lamb, 1 skewer of vegetables, and ⅓ cup rice.

Lettuce Slices With Radish Cream Dressing
Chopped radishes spend seasoning time in a tangy sour-cream dressing before coming to the table on lettuce.
Makes 6 servings, 33 calories each

> 2 bunches radishes, washed and trimmed
> 2 tablespoons low-calorie mayonnaise
> 2 tablespoons dairy sour cream
> 1 tablespoon skim milk
> ½ teaspoon salt
>   Freshly ground pepper
> 1 medium-size head iceberg lettuce

1 Chop radishes fine; drain well; place in a small bowl.
2 Stir in mayonnaise, sour cream, milk, salt, and pepper to taste. Let stand 15 minutes to season.
3 When ready to serve, cut lettuce into 6 even slices; place on salad plates; spoon radish mixture on top, dividing evenly.
Weight-watcher's serving: 1 slice lettuce with about 3 tablespoons radish dressing.

Chicken Chinese
Jellied Consommé (¾ cup per serving)
*Oriental Chicken and Vegetables with Rice
*Cabbage Relish Salads

Oriental Chicken and Vegetables
Diet dinner that definitely doesn't look it: Strips of all white meat and three vegetables in a ring of rice.
Makes 6 servings, 293 calories each

> 4 chicken breasts, weighing about 9 ounces each
> 1 teaspoon salt
> 1 package (about 10 ounces) frozen French-style green beans
> 1 cup diced celery
> 1 can (about 1 pound) bean sprouts, drained
>   Water
> 3 tablespoons cider vinegar
> ¼ teaspoon pepper
> 2 tablespoons cornstarch
> 3 tablespoons soy sauce
> 2 medium-size tomatoes, each cut in 6 wedges
> 3 cups hot cooked rice

1 Strip skin from chicken; cut meat from bones, then cut into ¼-inch-wide strips.
2 Sprinkle salt in a large frying pan. Add

chicken and sauté, stirring often, 10 minutes; push to one side.

3 Place frozen beans in frying pan; cook, breaking beans apart as they thaw, 5 minutes; stir in celery, bean sprouts, ¾ cup water, vinegar, and pepper. Heat to boiling; cover. Simmer 5 minutes.

4 Blend cornstarch with 2 tablespoons water until smooth in a cup; stir in soy sauce; stir into mixture in frying pan. Cook, stirring constantly, until mixture thickens and boils 3 minutes. Lay tomato wedges on top; cover again, steam 5 minutes, or just until tomatoes are heated through.

5 Spoon a ring of rice around edge of each of 6 heated serving plates; spoon chicken mixture into centers, placing tomato wedges on top.

Weight-watcher's serving: 1¼ cups chicken mixture, ½ cup rice, and 2 tomato wedges.

Cabbage Relish Salads

A great salad for slimmers, this crisply different coleslaw made with shredded Chinese cabbage and carrots.

Makes 6 servings, 34 calories each

1 small head Chinese cabbage
2 large carrots
3 tablespoons low-calorie mayonnaise
2 tablespoons skim milk
1 tablespoon cider vinegar
¼ teaspoon dry mustard
¼ teaspoon salt
⅛ teaspoon pepper
Granulated or liquid no-calorie sweetener
6 large lettuce leaves

1 Shred cabbage fine; wash and drain well. Place in a large bowl. Pare carrots and shred; add to cabbage.

2 Blend mayonnaise, milk, vinegar, mustard, salt, and pepper in a cup; stir in your favorite no-calorie sweetener, using the equivalent of 2 tablespoons sugar. Pour over cabbage mixture; toss lightly to mix.

3 Line 6 individual salad bowls with lettuce; spoon cabbage mixture in centers.

Weight-watcher's serving: 1 salad bowl or about 1¼ cups cabbage mixture.

Beef in the Round
*Meat Balls Scandia
Baked Potatoes (1 small per serving)
*Double Bean Salad Bowls

Meat Balls Scandia

Meat balls poach in a savory broth that holds the calorie line and becomes a superb base for gravy.

Makes 6 servings, 223 calories each

1¼ pounds lean ground round
½ cup soft white-bread crumbs (1 slice)
¼ cup skim milk
1 egg, separated
½ teaspoon grated lemon rind
1 tablespoon finely chopped onion
  Water
2 envelopes instant beef broth
  OR: 2 beef-flavor bouillon cubes
1 tablespoon all-purpose flour
2 tablespoons capers
1 tablespoon chopped parsley

1 Combine ground round, bread crumbs, milk, egg white, lemon rind, and onion in a medium-size bowl; mix lightly until well blended. Shape into 24 balls. Set egg yolk aside for Step 4.

2 Combine 6 cups water and beef broth or bouillon cubes in a large saucepan; heat to boiling. Add meat balls; cover. Simmer 20 minutes. Remove meat balls with a slotted spoon to a bowl; keep hot. Continue cooking broth rapidly until it is reduced to 2 cups.

3 Smooth flour and 2 tablespoons water to a paste in a cup; stir into the 2 cups boiling liquid. Cook, stirring constantly, until mixture thickens and boils 1 minute.

4 Beat egg yolk in a small bowl; slowly stir in about ½ cup of the hot mixture, then stir back into remaining mixture in saucepan; cook 1 minute longer. Stir in capers and parsley.

5 Place meat balls on a heated deep serving platter; spoon gravy over top. Or serve gravy separately to spoon over both meat and baked potatoes.

Weight-watcher's serving: 4 meat balls and about ⅓ cup gravy.

Double Bean Salad Bowls

For a change, make salad your first course. It's surprisingly filling, so you won't be as hungry for the rest of the meal.

Makes 6 servings, 48 calories each

1 package (9 ounces) frozen cut green beans
1 package (9 ounces) frozen wax beans

748

6 tablespoons bottled low-calorie French dressing
½ small head iceberg lettuce

1 Cook green and wax beans in separate saucepans, following label directions; drain, Place each in a small bowl; drizzle with 3 tablespoons of the salad dressing; toss lightly to mix. Chill at least an hour to season.
2 Just before serving, shred lettuce coarsely; place in 6 individual salad bowls. Spoon beans, dividing evenly, in separate piles on top. Garnish each salad with several small white onion rings, if you wish.
Weight-watcher's serving: 1 bowl.

COUNTDOWN DESSERTS

Lemon-Lime Sparkle
Two of the tangiest gelatin flavors snow-capped with whipped topping—a most refreshing way to stay slender!
Makes 6 servings, 19 calories each

3 bottles (10 ounces each) low-calorie citrus-flavor carbonated beverage
1 envelope (2 to a package) low-calorie lemon-flavor gelatin
1 envelope (2 to a package) low-calorie lime-flavor gelatin
1 envelope (2 to a package) low-calorie whipped-topping mix
Water
Vanilla

1 Heat 2 bottles of the carbonated beverage to boiling in a small saucepan; stir 1¼ cups into lemon gelatin until dissolved in a small bowl; stir remainder into lime gelatin in a second small bowl. Stir half of beverage in third bottle into mixture in each bowl.
2 Pour gelatin mixtures into separate pans, 9x9x2. Chill several hours, or until firm.
3 Just before serving, prepare whipped-topping mix with water and vanilla, following label directions.
4 Cut gelatin in each pan into ¼-inch cubes with a sharp knife. Spoon lemon into 6 parfait glasses, dividing evenly; spoon lime cubes on top. Garnish each glass with a spoonful of whipped topping; cover remainder and keep chilled to use another time.
Weight-watcher's serving: 1 parfait with 1 tablespoon whipped topping.

Molded Cheese Snow with Strawberries
In this translation of a French classic, all you'll miss is the calories. Any fresh fruit could stand in for strawberries.
Makes 6 servings, 82 calories each

1 container (12 ounces) pot cheese
⅓ cup skim milk
2 tablespoons dairy sour cream
1 teaspoon vanilla
 Granulated or liquid no-calorie sweetener
1 pint (2 cups) strawberries, washed, hulled, and halved

1 Combine pot cheese and skim milk in an electric-blender container; cover. Beat until smooth; pour into a medium-size bowl. (If you do not have a blender, press cheese through a sieve into a medium-size bowl; stir in skim milk.)
2 Stir in sour cream, vanilla, and your favorite no-calorie sweetener, using the equivalent of 2 tablespoons sugar.
3 Line 6 individual heart-shape or regular molds with cheesecloth large enough to hang over edge; pack cheese mixture into molds; fold cheesecloth over tops. Set molds in a pan for easy handling. Chill at least 3 hours.
4 When ready to serve, fold back cheesecloth; invert molds onto serving plates; peel off cloth. Arrange strawberries around molds, placing a whole one on top, if you wish.
Weight-watcher's serving: 1 mold and about ⅓ cup strawberries.

Double Orange Coupe
Velvety-smooth, fresh fruit cream looks and tastes twice as inviting when you serve it in orange "cups."
Make 6 servings, 87 calories each

6 large oranges
⅓ cup cornstarch
 Granulated, liquid, or tablet no-calorie sweetener
½ teaspoon grated lemon rind
1 teaspoon lemon juice
3 egg whites
2 tablespoons granulated sugar

1 Halve oranges crosswise; squeeze juice, being careful not to break shells. Measure 2 cups of the juice, then chill any remainder to use another time. Pick out 6 of the prettiest

749

Glazed Fruit Meringues, Double Orange Coupe.

shells to use for servers; scoop out membranes. Discard remaining shells.

2 Blend the 2 cups orange juice with cornstarch until smooth in a medium-size saucepan; stir in your favorite no-calorie sweetener, using the equivalent of 8 tablespoons sugar. Cook, stirring constantly, until mixture thickens and boils 3 minutes; remove from heat. Cool slightly; stir in lemon rind and juice.

3 Beat egg whites until foamy-white and double in volume in a medium-size bowl; beat in sugar until meringue stands in firm peaks. Fold into warm orange mixture.

750

4 Place orange shells in 6 sherbet glasses; spoon orange mixture into shells. Chill at least an hour, or until serving time. Garnish each with a sprig of fresh mint, if you wish.

Weight-watcher's serving: 1 filled orange half.

Glazed Fruit Meringues

Miniatures fancy enough for the fussiest company, to keep in mind when you're entertaining calorie-conscious friends.

Bake at 250° for 1 hour. Makes 8 servings, 58 calories each

2 egg whites
1 teaspoon lemon juice
⅓ cup sugar
1 teaspoon vanilla
2 teaspoons cornstarch
  Dash of ground cardamom
1 can (1 pound) diet-pack fruits for salad
  Red food coloring

1 Line a large cookie sheet with brown paper; draw 16 two-inch rounds, 2 inches apart, on paper. (A regular water glass makes a handy pattern.)

2 Beat egg whites with lemon juice until foamy-white and double in volume in a small bowl. Sprinkle in sugar, 1 tablespoon at a time, beating all the time until sugar completely dissolves and meringue stands in firm peaks; beat in vanilla.

3 Attach a fancy tip to a pastry bag; spoon meringue into bag. Starting at centers of rounds drawn on paper, press out meringue in circles, building up outer edge to form small shells. (If you do not have a pastry bag, spread 2 tablespoons meringue onto each circle, building up edge.)

4 Bake in very slow oven (250°) 1 hour, or until delicately golden. Cool on cookie sheet 5 minutes; loosen carefully from paper with a spatula; place on wire racks to cool.

5 About an hour before serving, mix cornstarch and cardamom in a small saucepan. Drain syrup from fruits and blend into cornstarch mixture until smooth.

6 Cook, stirring constantly, until mixture thickens and boils 3 minutes; remove from heat. Stir in a drop or two food coloring to tint rosy red; cool.

7 Halve any large pieces of fruit; arrange pieces in meringue shells. Brush fruits with tinted syrup to glaze lightly.

Weight-watcher's serving: 2 filled meringue shells.

●

Blushing Pear Square

Beneath the mellow poached fruit, a brown-sugar sponge layer; pink plus on the surface is a cranberry glaze.

Bake at 325° for 25 minutes. Makes 12 servings, 104 calories each

¾ cup sifted cake flour
1 teaspoon baking powder
½ teaspoon pumpkin-pie spice
¼ teaspoon salt
2 eggs
⅓ cup granulated sugar
¼ cup firmly packed light brown sugar
¼ cup boiling water
  BLUSHING PEARS (recipe follows)

1 Sift cake flour, baking powder, pumpkin-pie spice, and salt onto wax paper.

2 Separate eggs, placing whites in a medium-size bowl and yolks in a small bowl.

3 Beat egg whites until foamy-white and double in volume; beat in granulated sugar, 1 tablespoon at a time, until meringue forms soft peaks.

4 Beat egg yolks until fluffy-thick; beat in brown sugar, 1 tablespoon at a time. Stir in boiling water; beat vigorously 5 minutes, or until mixture forms soft peaks.

5 Fold egg-yolk mixture into egg-white mixture until no streaks of yellow remain; fold in flour mixture, one-fourth at a time. Pour batter into an ungreased baking pan, 9x9x2.

6 Bake in slow oven (325°) 25 minutes, or until top springs back when lightly pressed with fingertip. Cool completely in pan on a wire rack.

7 While cake cools, fix BLUSHING PEARS (*recipe follows*).

8 Loosen cake around edges with a knife; turn out, then turn right side up on a serving plate. Lift pears from syrup and arrange in a pattern on top of cake; spoon syrup evenly over all. Cut into 12 serving-size pieces.

BLUSHING PEARS—Pare 3 medium-size firm ripe pears; quarter and core. Place pears and ¾ cup low-calorie cranberry-juice cocktail in a medium-size frying pan. Heat to boiling, then simmer, turning pears several times, 10 minutes, or until tender. Blend 1 tablespoon cornstarch and ¼ cup more cranberry-juice cocktail until smooth in a cup; stir into liquid in frying pan. Cook, stirring constantly, until mixture thickens and boils 3 minutes; remove from heat; cool.

Weight-watcher's serving: 1 piece of cake with 1 pear quarter and syrup.

Pineapple Puff

Your refrigerator ''bakes'' this cool concoction; pineapple packed in pure juice gives it fresh fruit flavor.

Makes 8 servings, 113 calories each

4 eggs, separated
1 can (1 pound, 4 ounces) crushed pineapple in pure juice
  Granulated, liquid, or tablet no-calorie sweetener
2 envelopes unflavored gelatin
¾ cup instant nonfat dry milk
¾ cup ice water

1 Prepare a 4-cup soufflé dish this way: Cut a strip of foil, 12 inches wide and long enough to go around dish with a 1-inch overlap; fold in half lengthwise. Wrap around dish to make a 2-inch stand-up collar; hold in place with a rubber band and a paper clip.

2 Beat egg yolks in the top of a double boiler; stir in pineapple and juice and your favorite no-calorie sweetener, using the equivalent of 8 tablespoons sugar. Sprinkle gelatin over top; let stand several minutes to soften gelatin. Place top of double boiler over simmering water.

3 Cook, stirring constantly, 15 minutes, or until gelatin dissolves and mixture coats a spoon; pour into a large bowl.

4 Set bowl in a pan of ice and water; chill, stirring several times, just until as thick as unbeaten egg white.

5 While pineapple mixture chills, beat egg

Every dieter's best friends: tall, quivery, shimmering gelatin molds made with slimming low-calorie gelatins.

whites just until they form soft peaks in a medium-size bowl.

6 Sprinkle dry milk powder over ice water in a chilled medium-size bowl; beat with an electric beater at high speed until stiff.

7 Fold beaten egg whites, then whipped milk into thickened gelatin mixture, keeping bowl over ice, until no streaks of white remain. Pour into prepared soufflé dish. Chill several hours, or until firm. Spoon into serving dishes; garnish each with a sprig of mint, if you wish.
Weight-watcher's serving: 1 cup.

●

French Fruit Pie
With its pudding base and double-fruit crown, it's hard to believe this pie is the kind that's kind to your figure!
Bake shell at 400° for 15 minutes. Makes 8 servings, 160 calories each

LOW-CALORIE PASTRY *(recipe follows)*
1 envelope (2 to a package) low-calorie vanilla pudding and pie-filling mix
1 cup skim milk
1 can (1 pound) diet-pack cling peach slices
1 can (about 9 ounces) diet-pack pineapple tidbits
1 tablespoon cornstarch
1 teaspoon orange extract

1 Make LOW-CALORIE PASTRY. Roll out to a 12-inch round between two sheets of wax paper (no flour needed); fit into a 9-inch pie plate. Trim overhang to ½ inch; turn edge under, flush with rim; flute. Prick shell well all over with a fork.

2 Bake in hot oven (400°) 15 minutes, or until golden. Cool completely on a wire rack.

3 Prepare pudding mix with the 1 cup skim milk, following label directions; chill.

4 Drain liquids from peaches and pineapple into a cup, then blend into cornstarch until smooth in a small saucepan. Cook, stirring constantly,

until glaze thickens and boil 3 minutes; remove from heat. Stir in orange extract; cool.

5 Spread chilled pudding into cooled pastry shell; arrange peaches and pineapple in a pattern on top. Spoon glaze over fruits. Chill until glaze sets.

LOW-CALORIE PASTRY—Combine ½ cup sifted all-purpose flour and ½ teaspoon salt in a medium-size bowl. Cut in 4 tablespoons (½ stick) margarine with a pastry blender, then blend in another ½ cup sifted all-purpose flour until mixture is crumbly. Sprinkle 7 teaspoons ice water, part at a time, over mixture; mix lightly with a fork just until pastry holds together and leaves side of bowl clean. Makes enough for one 9-inch shell.
Weight-watcher's serving: ⅛ wedge of pie.

●

Chocolate-Almond Roll
Weight-watchers can have their cake, plus chocolate pudding and even almonds, at the cost of few calories.
Bake at 400° for 8 minutes. Makes 10 servings, 112 calories each

½ cup sifted cake flour
¾ teaspoon baking powder
¼ teaspoon salt
3 eggs
½ cup granulated sugar
1 teaspoon almond extract
1 tablespoon 10X (confectioners' powdered) sugar
1 envelope (2 to a package) low-calorie Chocolate pudding and pie-filling mix
1½ cups skim milk
2 tablespoons toasted slivered almonds

1 Grease a baking pan, 15x10x1; line bottom with wax paper; grease paper.

2 Measure flour, baking powder, and salt into sifter.

3 Beat eggs until foamy-light and double in

volume in a large bowl; beat in granulated sugar, 1 tablespoon at a time, until mixture is thick; stir in almond extract.

4 Sift flour mixture over top, then fold in; pour into prepared pan.

5 Bake in hot oven (400°) 8 minutes, or until center springs back when lightly pressed with fingertip. Loosen cake around edges with a knife; invert onto a towel dusted with the 1 tablespoon 10X sugar; peel off wax paper. Trim crisp edges from cake. Starting at a short end, roll up cake, jelly-roll fashion; cool completely.

6 Prepare pudding mix with the 1½ cups skim milk, following label directions; chill.

7 Unroll cake carefully. Spread with all but ½ cup of the pudding; reroll. Place on serving plate; chill.

8 Just before serving, spread saved ½ cup pudding in a ribbon over cake; sprinkle with almonds. Cut cake crosswise into 10 slices.
Weight-watcher's serving: 1 slice.

Choco-Chip Pear Velvet
Creamy yogurt is the secret to its low calories and satiny smoothness.
Makes 6 servings

    1 egg
    ½ cup water
      Dash of salt
      Granulated or liquid no-calorie sweetener
    1 envelope unflavored gelatin
    3 tablespoons instant nonfat dry milk
    1 teaspoon vanilla
    2 containers (8 ounces each) vanilla yogurt
    1 can (about 1 pound) diet-pack quartered
      pears, drained
    1 tablespoon grated sweet cooking chocolate
      (from a 4-ounce bar)

1 Separate egg into 2 small bowls. Beat yolk slightly; beat in water and salt. Sweeten with

your favorite no-calorie sweetener, using the equivalent of 24 teaspoons (½ cup) sugar.

2 Mix gelatin and dry milk in top of double boiler; stir in egg-yolk mixture.

3 Cook, stirring constantly, over simmering water, 5 minutes, or until gelatin dissolves and mixture coats a metal spoon. Strain into a large bowl; stir in vanilla.

4 Chill 30 minutes, or just until mixture is as thick as unbeaten egg white; blend in yogurt until creamy-smooth.

5 Beat egg white until it forms soft peaks; fold into yogurt mixture. Pour into a 4-cup shallow mold or an 8x1½-inch layer-cake pan. Chill 3 to 4 hours, or until firm.

6 To unmold, run a sharp-tip, thin-blade knife around top of mold, then dip mold very quickly

753

in and out of a pan of hot water. Invert onto chilled serving plate; lift off mold. Arrange pear quarters in a ring on top; sprinkle with grated chocolate. Cut into 6 wedges.
Dieter's portion: 1 wedge or 1/6 of mold—108 calories.

●

Banana Bounty Pie
Calorie watchers and nondieters, too, will go for this sweet reward.
Bake at 425° for 15 minutes. Makes one 9-inch pie

      LOW-CALORIE PASTRY SHELL *(recipe follows)*
6 tablespoons flaked coconut
3 eggs, separated
½ cup skim milk
½ cup water
1 envelope unflavored gelatin
1 teaspoon vanilla
   Granulated or liquid no-calorie sweetener
1 medium-size banana, peeled and sliced thin

1 Mix, bake, and cool LOW-CALORIE PASTRY SHELL. Turn off oven heat.
2 Spread coconut in a pie plate; toast in heated oven 5 minutes, or until golden. (Watch it, for it browns quickly.) Set aside for Step 6.
3 Beat egg yolks with milk and water until blended in top of double boiler; stir in gelatin.
4 Cook, stirring constantly, over hot, *not boiling,* water 7 minutes, or until gelatin dissolves and mixture coats a metal spoon; remove from heat.
5 Stir in vanilla and your favorite no-calorie sweetener, using the equivalent of 24 teaspoons (½ cup) sugar. Chill 30 minutes, or until as thick as unbeaten egg white.
6 Beat egg whites until they form soft peaks in medium-size bowl. Gradually fold in thickened gelatin mixture and 4 tablespoons of the toasted coconut until no streaks of white remain. (Save remaining coconut for topping in Step 8.)
7 Spoon filling into cooled pastry shell. Chill several hours, or until firm.
8 When ready to serve, top with a ring of banana slices; mound saved coconut in center. Cut into 8 even-size wedges.
Dieter's portion: 1 wedge or ⅛ of pie—167 calories.

Low-Calorie Pastry Shell
Bake at 425° for 15 minutes. Makes one 9-inch pie shell

1 cup sifted all-purpose flour
½ teaspoon salt
4 tablespoons (½ stick) margarine
2½ tablespoons ice water

1 Sift ½ cup flour and salt into medium-size bowl; cut in margarine with pastry blender until mixture is crumbly, then blend in remaining ½ cup sifted flour until crumbly.
2 Sprinkle ice water over, 1 tablespoon at a time; mix lightly with a fork just until pastry holds together and leaves side of bowl clean.
3 Roll out to a 12-inch round between 2 sheets of wax paper (no flour needed); fit into a 9-inch pie plate. Trim overhang to ½ inch; turn under flush with rim; flute. Prick well all over with a fork.
4 Bake in hot oven (425°) 15 minutes, or until golden. Cool completely on wire rack.

●

Lemon Cheesecake Tower
Shimmery layer of gelatin crowns a creamy no-bake cheesecake for this favorite.
Makes 12 servings

2 eggs
1 cup water
¼ teaspoon salt
   Granulated or liquid no-calorie sweetener
3 envelopes unflavored gelatin
⅓ cup instant nonfat dry milk
1 teaspoon grated lemon peel
3 tablespoons lemon juice
1 teaspoon vanilla
2 envelopes low-calorie lemon-flavor gelatin (3 to a package)
   Green food coloring
3 cups (1½ pounds) cream-style cottage cheese
1 cup evaporated milk, well-chilled

1 Separate eggs, putting whites in a small bowl, yolks in a second small bowl. Beat egg yolks slightly with water and salt; sweeten with your favorite no-calorie sweetener, using the equivalent of 1 cup (48 teaspoons) sugar.
2 Mix unflavored gelatin and milk powder in top of a small double boiler; stir in egg-yolk mixture. Cook, stirring constantly, over hot, *not boiling,* water 5 minutes, or until gelatin dissolves and mixture coats a metal spoon; remove from heat.
3 Strain into a large bowl; stir in lemon peel, 2 tablespoons of the lemon juice, and vanilla. (Save remaining 1 tablespoon lemon juice for Step 6.) Chill 30 minutes, or just until as thick as unbeaten egg white.
4 While gelatin-custard mixture chills, prepare lemon-flavor gelatin, following label directions; tint lightly with a drop or two of green food

Yes, this creamy-rich Lemon Cheesecake Tower is actually low in calories, a truly slimming 123 per serving.

Deceptively diet-fare: pastel pink Frozen Strawberry "Cream" and light-as-a-cloud Daffodil Ring made of angel food cake.

coloring. Pour into a 10-cup tall mold. Chill 20 minutes, or *just* until sticky-firm.

5 Press cottage cheese through a sieve into a medium-size bowl; stir into thickened gelatin-custard mixture from Step 3.

6 Beat egg whites until they stand in firm peaks. Beat well-chilled evaporated milk with saved 1 tablespoon lemon juice until stiff in a small bowl.

7 Fold beaten egg whites, then whipped milk into gelatin-cheese mixture; pour over *sticky-firm layer* in mold. Chill at least 4 hours, or until firm.

8 To unmold, run a sharp-tip, thin-blade knife around top of mold, then dip mold *very quickly* in and out of a pan of hot water. Cover mold with serving plate; turn upside down; carefully lift off mold. Garnish with a small cluster of green grapes, if you wish. Cut into wedges.
Dieter's portion: 1 wedge (1/12 of mold)—123 calories.

756

●

Frozen Strawberry "Cream"
Recipe makes about 12 cups—enough for a billowy sweet pie treat and a mousselike dessert for another day.
Bake pie shell at 375° for 8 minutes. Makes 8 servings

1 cup zwieback crumbs (about 12 slices)
1 teaspoon ground cinnamon
2 tablespoons melted butter or margarine
  Liquid no-calorie sweetener
2 cups (1 pint) fresh strawberries
1 egg white
1 cup sugar

1 Make shell: Mix crumbs and cinnamon in small bowl. Combine melted butter or margarine and your favorite no-calorie sweetener, using the equivalent of 6 teaspoons sugar, in a cup; blend into crumb mixture. Press evenly over bottom and side of a 9-inch pie plate.

2 Bake in moderate oven (375°) 8 minutes; cool completely on a wire rack.

3 Make "cream": Wash, hull, and halve strawberries. Combine with egg white and sugar in the large bowl of electric mixer; beat at medium speed 10 minutes, or until mixture turns into a billowy pink fluff that nearly fills bowl.

4 Measure out 6 cups and spoon into cooled crust, swirling to a peak in center. Spoon remaining into 2 ice-cube trays or a pan, 8x8x2; cover with transparent wrap or foil.

5 Freeze pie 3 hours, or until firm. Freeze dessert in trays 3 hours, or until ready to use.

6 Serve pie plain, or garnish with halved strawberries placed in a ring around edge, if you wish.
Dieter's portion: 1 wedge (⅛ of pie) with no garnish—136 calories. With 1 halved strawberry for garnish—140 calories. One-half cup of frozen dessert—41 calories.

Daffodil Ring

It's a double treat—airy-light angel food and spongecake.
Bake at 325° for 30 minutes. Makes one 9-inch ring cake

¾ cup sifted cake flour
½ teaspoon salt
3 eggs, separated
½ teaspoon cream of tartar
⅔ cup sugar
1 teaspoon vanilla
3 tablespoons hot water
1 teaspoon orange extract
1 tablespoon 10X (confectioners' powdered) sugar

1 Sift flour and salt onto wax paper or foil.
2 Beat egg whites with cream of tartar until foamy-white and double in volume in a large bowl. Sprinkle in ⅓ cup of the granulated sugar *very slowly,* 1 tablespoon at a time, beating all the time until meringue stands in firm peaks; beat in vanilla. (Save remaining ⅓ cup sugar for Step 4.)
3 Sprinkle 2 tablespoons of the flour mixture over top; fold in completely. Repeat with 4 tablespoons more flour mixture. (Save remaining 6 tablespoons flour for Step 5.)
4 Beat egg yolks with hot *(not boiling)* water until very thick and light lemon color in a medium-size bowl. Sprinkle in saved ⅓ cup granulated sugar, 1 tablespoon at a time, beating all the time, until mixture is creamy-thick; beat in orange extract.
5 Sprinkle 2 tablespoons of the remaining flour mixture over top of egg-yolk mixture; fold in completely. Repeat with remaining flour mixture.
6 Spoon batters, alternating spoonfuls of white and yellow, into an ungreased 9-inch ring mold. (Do not stir batters in pan.)
7 Bake in slow oven (325°) 30 minutes, or until golden and top springs back when lightly pressed with fingertip.
8 Turn cake in pan upside down on a wire rack; cool completely. When ready to unmold, loosen around edge and center with knife; invert onto serving plate. Sprinkle 10X sugar over top. Slice into 10 even-size wedges to serve plain. Or, if you wish, fill a small serving bowl with diet-pack apricot halves and set bowl in center of cake.
Dieter's portion: 1 wedge (1/10 of cake)—103 calories. Count 10 calories for 2 diet-pack apricot halves.

Coffee Sparkle

All you can pile into a parfait glass adds up to a real bargain in calories.
Makes 6 servings

2 envelopes unflavored gelatin
½ cup cold water
3½ cups freshly brewed strong coffee
Granulated or liquid no-calorie sweetener
½ teaspoon vanilla
Dash of salt
DIETER'S WHIPPED CREAM (recipe follows)

1 Soften gelatin in cold water in medium-size bowl; stir in hot coffee until gelatin dissolves. Sweeten with your favorite no-calorie sweetener, using the equivalent of 16 teaspoons (⅓ cup) sugar; stir in vanilla and salt.
2 Pour into shallow pan, 8x8x2; chill 2 hours, or until firm. Break gelatin up with a fork or press through a potato ricer into a medium-size bowl.
3 Spoon into 6 parfait glasses, dividing evenly; top each with 1 tablespoon DIETER'S WHIPPED CREAM. Garnish with an orange twist, if you wish. (To make, cut 6 thin ribbons from rind of an orange; tie each in a loose knot.)
DIETER'S WHIPPED CREAM—Beat 3 tablespoons cream for whipping until stiff in a small bowl. Serve plain or sweeten to taste with your favorite liquid no-calorie sweetener. Makes about ⅓ cup.
Dieter's portion: 1 parfait glass with 1 tablespoon whipped cream—39 calories. Without whipped-cream topping—12 calories.

Ginger Fruit Compote

Ginger ale adds a fizzy tang, but no calories, to fresh pineapple and orange sections.
Makes 6 servings

6 medium-size oranges
¼ small ripe pineapple, cut lengthwise
1 cup no-calorie ginger ale

1 Pare and section oranges, working over a medium-size bowl to catch the juice.
2 Cut core from pineapple; slice fruit into ¼-inch-thick fan-shape pieces, then pare.
3 Place pineapple fans in bowl with oranges; chill until serving time.
4 Spoon into 6 dessert dishes, dividing evenly; pour ginger ale over. Garnish each with a sprig of mint, if you wish.
Dieter's portion: 1 dessert dish, or about 1 cupful—98 calories.

Lemon-Lime Puff

Two popular flavors accent each other in this sweet, fluffy-light top-off.
Bake at 350° for 35 minutes. Makes 6 servings

4 eggs
¼ teaspoon salt
4 tablespoons sugar
1 teaspoon grated lemon peel
½ teaspoon grated lime peel
2 tablespoons lemon juice
1 tablespoon lime juice

1 Separate eggs, putting whites in a large bowl, yolks in a medium-size bowl.
2 Beat egg whites with salt until foamy-white and double in volume. Sprinkle in 2 tablespoons of the sugar *very slowly*, beating all the time until meringue forms soft peaks.
3 Beat egg yolks until thick and lemon-color; beat in remaining 2 tablespoons sugar, then remaining ingredients, beating about 1 minute longer, or until slightly thickened. Fold into beaten egg whites until no streaks of yellow or white remain.
4 Spoon into an ungreased 4-cup soufflé dish or straight-side baking dish; set dish in a shallow pan. Place pan on oven shelf; pour boiling water into pan to depth of about an inch.
5 Bake in moderate oven (350°) 35 minutes, or until puffy-light and firm in center. Serve at once.
Dieter's portion: 1 dessert dish, (1/6 of the baked puff)—90 calories.

Lemon-Lime Royale

Fresh fruits crown shimmering gelatin in this inviting diet top-off.
Makes 6 servings

2 envelopes low-calorie lemon-flavor gelatin (3 to a package)
2 cups hot water
6 thin slices fresh lime
1 medium-size grapefruit
2 oranges

1 Dissolve gelatin in hot water in medium-size bowl; chill until as thick as unbeaten egg white.
2 Spoon into 6 parfait glasses, dividing evenly. Carefully stand a lime slice in center of gelatin in each glass; chill until firm.
3 Pare and section grapefruit and oranges into a small bowl; chill. When ready to serve, drain off juices and save for breakfast beverage. Spoon fruits on top of gelatin, dividing evenly. Garnish with a thin orange slice, if you wish.
Dieter's portion: 1 parfait glass—45 calories.

SNACKTIME TREATS FOR DIETERS

- **Fresh vegetable nibbles**—Keep raw cauliflowerets, celery, cucumber, carrot, green pepper, radishes, or lettuce fixed and handy in your refrigerator. All you want at one time won't add up to more than 25 calories.
- **Mushrooms**—Slice unpeeled fresh ones, or open a can of mushroom caps and drain, then dip into seasoned salt, lightly salted lemon juice, or chopped parsley or watercress. The calorie count—about 14 for six fresh ones and 20 in a small can—is a weight-watcher's true friend.
- **Skim milk or buttermilk**—Perfect for an afternoon or before-bedtime pickup—and so good for you, too. Count 90 calories for a cupful. Munch on five thin pretzel sticks as a go-with for only 20 calories.
- **Fresh fruits**—Want to splurge just a bit? Treat yourself to ½ cup strawberries to eat plain for 28 calories, or dip into ¼ cup creamy yogurt for just 35 more. Grapes taste equally satisfying served this way and ½ cupful equals 48 calories. Remember that half a medium-size apple can be yours for just 35 calories. Or slice it and spread with 2 tablespoons cottage cheese (the dry kind) and figure 25 more. And either a small grapefruit half or large orange saved from breakfast to enjoy at midmorning counts just 65 calories.
- **Tomato juice, beef broth**—Enjoy a cupful of tomato juice for 45 calories or stir in one envelope unflavored gelatine for extra protein and a plus of 28 calories. (To fix, sprinkle gelatin into juice to soften, then stir in and sip cold. Or heat just until the gelatin dissolves.) Condensed beef broth poured right from the can over ice, or diluted with an equal amount of water, counts a low 17 calories for ⅔ cup. Two saltines to eat with it add 35 calories.

AROUND-THE-CLOCK REFRESHERS —ALL CALORIE-FREE

- **No-Calorie Beverages**—Check the many kinds your supermarket offers, including presweetened (but sugar-free) mixes in handy foil envelopes.

- **Bouillon**—Make it with cubes, paste, or the instant variety in envelopes to enjoy hot in midmorning, afternoon, or late evening.

- **Tea and coffee**—Serve either hot or iced—but no sugar, milk, or cream, please. To tea add fresh lemon for a flavor spark but no calories.

A fantastic bit of magic, a dessert that actually contains fewer calories than an orange, an apple, half a grapefruit. It's Coffee Sparkle, 39 calories per serving.

More magic, another dessert weighing in lighter than most fruits. This one is Lemon-Lime Royale at 45 calories.

YOUR CALORIE COUNTER

FOOD	AMOUNT	COUNT
A		
Almonds, shelled	1 cup	850
salted	10 nuts	83
salted, chopped	1 tbsp.	58
Anchovies, canned fillets	4 fillets	28
Angel cake, see Cakes		
Apple	1 medium (2½'')	70
Apple butter	1 tbsp.	33
Apple juice, bottled or		
canned	1 cup	120
Applesauce, canned		
sweetened	1 cup	230
unsweetened or diet-pack	1 cup	100
Apricots		
fresh	3	55
canned, halves in		
heavy syrup	½ cup	110
canned, diet-pack	½ cup	39
dried	10 halves	90
Apricot nectar, canned	1 cup	140
Artichokes		
fresh, cooked	1 medium	30
frozen, hearts, cooked	½ cup	22
Asparagus		
fresh, cooked	6 spears	20
canned	6 spears	20
frozen, cut, cooked	½ cup	18
frozen, spears, cooked	5	23
Avocado	½ medium (3'' long)	245
	½ cup cubes	186

FOOD	AMOUNT	COUNT
B		
Bacon		
broiled or fried, crisp	2 slices	100
Canadian, lean, broiled	3 slices	50
Bamboo shoots, canned	1 cup	41
Banana	1 (6'' long)	85
Barley, pearl		
cooked	1 cup	142
uncooked	¼ cup	177
Bean sprouts, canned	½ cup	20
Beans		
baked, with pork		
and molasses	1 cup	325
baked, with pork		
and tomato sauce	1 cup	295
green		
fresh, cut, cooked	½ cup	15
canned, cut	½ cup	14
frozen, cut, cooked	½ cup	18
Italian		
frozen, cooked	½ cup	23
kidney, canned	1 cup	230
lima		
baby		
fresh, cooked	1 cup	180
frozen, cooked	½ cup	94
dried, large, cooked	1 cup	260
Fordhook, frozen, cooked	½ cup	90
wax		
fresh, cooked	½ cup	15
canned	½ cup	15
frozen, cooked	½ cup	22

Beef		
brisket, fresh	1 slice (7''x1¼''x½'')	266
corned	1 slice (7''x1¼''x½'')	266
pot roast, blade	1 slice (4''x3''x⅝'')	506
roast		
rib	1 slice (5''x3½''x¼'')	243
rump	1 slice (5''x5''x¼'')	235
sirloin	1 slice (5''x5''x¼'')	186
steak		
club	12 oz. raw	793
cubed	6 oz. raw	305
flank	3 pieces (each 5''x1½''x¼'')	200
porterhouse	1 piece (4''x3''x1'')	412
round	1 piece (6''x4''x½'')	406
ground, raw	6 oz.	271
sirloin	1 piece (4''x3''x1'')	353
stew meat, chuck, boneless, raw	4 oz.	421
Beef and vegetable stew, canned	1 cup	210
Beef broth		
canned, condensed, undiluted	1 can	66
cubes	1	6
instant	1 envelope	8
Beef, canned, corned beef	3 oz.	185
Beef hash, canned, corned	3 oz.	155
Beef potpie, frozen	8 oz.	420
Beef TV dinner	1 dinner	380
Beer	1 cup	100
Beets, fresh, cooked diced	1 cup	50
Biscuits, baking powder	1 (2½'')	129
Blackberries		
fresh	½ cup	43
canned, diet-pack	½ cup	52
Blueberries		
fresh	½ cup	43
canned, diet-pack	½ cup	45
frozen, sweetened	½ cup	129
frozen, unsweetened	½ cup	45
Bologna	1 slice (4'' diameter x⅛'' thick)	87
Bouillon, see beef broth and chicken broth		
Bran flakes, 40%	¾ cup	95
Brandy	1½ oz.	75
Brazil nuts, shelled	4	100
Bread		
Boston brown	1 slice	100
cracked-wheat	1 slice	60
French or Italian	1 piece (2'')	108
pumpernickel	1 slice (3¾''x3¾''x⅛'')	65
raisin, unfrosted	1 slice	60
rye	1 slice (2¾''x2¼''x½'')	55
white, enriched	1 slice	60
whole-wheat	1 slice	55
Bread crumbs		
dry	1 cup	345
soft	1 cup	120
Broccoli		
fresh, spears, cooked	4	40
frozen, chopped, cooked	½ cup	25
frozen, spears, cooked	2 to 3	26
Brownies	1 (1½''x1½''x¾'')	120

Brussels sprouts		
fresh, cooked	1 cup	45
frozen, cooked	½ cup	29
Butter	1 tbsp.	100
Buttermilk, from skim milk	1 cup	90

C

Cabbage		
raw, finely shredded	1 cup	25
cooked, finely shredded	1 cup	35
Cabbage, Chinese		
raw, chopped	1 cup	15
cooked, chopped	1 cup	20
Cakes		
angel	1 two-inch wedge (from an 8″ cake)	110
chocolate, chocolate icing	1 two-inch wedge (from a 10″ cake)	445
cupcake, with chocolate icing	1 (2¾″ diameter)	185
plain cake, without icing	1 piece (3″x2″x1½″)	200
poundcake	1 slice	140
spongecake	1 two-inch wedge (from an 8″ cake)	120
Candy		
almonds, chocolate-covered	6	102
caramels	1	42
chocolate creams	1	47
chocolate fudge	1 piece (1¼″x1¼″x ½″)	66
chocolate-mint patty	1 (1⅜″ diameter)	40
marshmallows	1 large	26
peanut brittle	1 piece (2½″x1½″x ⅜″)	125
Cantaloupe	½ medium	60
balls	½ cup	20
Carbonated beverages	7-oz. bottle	80
Carrots		
raw, whole	1 (5″x1″)	20
raw, grated	1 cup	45
cooked, diced	1 cup	45
frozen, sliced, cooked	1 cup	45
Cashew nuts, roasted	8	164
Catsup	1 tbsp.	15
Cauliflower		
raw, flowerets	1 cup	25
cooked, flowerets	1 cup	25
frozen, flowerets, cooked	½ cup	15
Celery		
raw, diced	1 cup	15
raw, stalk	1	5
cooked, diced	½ cup	12
Cheese		
blue or Roquefort	1 oz.	105
Camembert	1 oz.	86
Cheddar or American	1-inch cube	70
grated	1 cup	445
grated	1 tbsp.	30
process	1-oz. slice	105
cottage, skim milk		
cream-style	1 cup	240
	1 oz.	30
dry	1 cup	195
	1 oz.	25
cream	1 oz.	105
	1 tbsp.	55
Parmesan, grated	1 tbsp.	31

Swiss		
natural	1 slice (7″x4″x⅛″)	168
process	1-oz. slice	105
Cheese foods, Cheddar	1 oz.	90
Cheese spreads	1 tbsp.	35
Cherries, sour, red		
canned	1 cup	230
Cherries, sweet		
fresh	1 cup	80
canned, sweetened	½ cup	112
canned, diet-pack	1 cup	134
Chicken		
broiled	½ broiler(¾ lb. raw)	248
fried	½ breast	201
fried	1 drumstick	101
roast	½ breast	200
roast	1 drumstick	101
roast	1 thigh	147
Chicken broth		
canned	14-oz. can	74
cubes	1	6
instant	1 envelope	10
Chicken livers	¼ lb.	146
Chicken potpie, frozen	8 oz.	490
Chicken soup, see Soups		
Chicken TV dinner	1 dinner	500
Chili con carne, canned		
with beans	1 cup	335
without beans	1 cup	510
Chili sauce	1 tbsp.	17
Chocolate		
unsweetened	1 oz. (1 square)	145
semisweet	1 oz. (1 square)	130
semisweet pieces	6-oz. package	906
sweet cooking	1 oz.	150
Chocolate bar, milk, plain	1 oz.	150
Chocolate malted milk		
shake with ice cream	1½ cups	500
Chocolate milk, commercial	1 cup	205
Chocolate syrup, thin	1 tbsp.	50
Clams		
raw, meat only	6 large	65
canned, clams and liquid	4 large (½ cup)	45
Clam juice	1 cup	35
Cocoa, with whole milk	1 cup	235
Cocoa powder	1 tbsp.	21
Coconut		
fresh	1 piece (2″x2″x½″)	161
shredded	1 cup	335
dried, shredded, sweetened	1 cup	340
Cod		
fresh, poached	1 piece (3″x3″x1″)	84
frozen, fillets, poached	4 oz.	84
frozen, sticks, breaded	5	276
Cola	1 cup	95
Cookies		
chocolate wafer	1 (2⅜″ diameter)	36
creme sandwich, chocolate	1	54
fig bars, small	1	55
gingersnaps	1 (3″ diameter)	52
sugar wafer	1 (2″x¾″x¼″)	10
vanilla wafer	1 large	22
Corn flakes		
plain	1 cup	100
presweetened	¾ cup	110
Corn, sweet		
fresh, cooked	1 ear (5″x1¾″)	70

canned, cream-style	½ cup	92
canned, whole-kernel	½ cup	70
frozen, whole-kernel, cooked	½ cup	73
frozen, on the cob, cooked	1 ear	100
Corn meal, white or yellow, dry	1 cup	420
Corn muffins	1 (2¾″ diameter)	150
Corn oil	1 tbsp.	125
Corn syrup, light or dark	1 tbsp.	60
Cornstarch	1 tbsp.	30
Cornstarch pudding, with whole milk		
chocolate	½ cup	189
vanilla	½ cup	138
low-calorie, with skim milk		
chocolate	½ cup	57
vanilla or butterscotch	½ cup	55
instant		
chocolate	½ cup	183
vanilla or butterscotch	½ cup	170
Cottonseed oil	1 tbsp.	125
Crab meat		
canned	3 oz.	85
frozen	3 oz.	89
Cracker meal	1 tbsp.	45
Crackers		
cheese	10 (1″ square)	34
graham		
plain	1 (2¼″ square)	30
chocolate-covered	1 (2″ square)	56
oyster	20	60
peanut-butter sandwich	1	45
pretzels	5 thin sticks (2″ long)	7
rye wafers	1 (3½″x1¾″)	21
saltines	1 (2″ square)	14
soda	1 (2½″ square)	23
Cranberry juice cocktail, bottled	1 cup	160
Cranberry sauce, sweetened, canned		
jellied or whole-berry	1 tbsp.	26
diet-pack	1 tbsp.	3
Cream		
half-and-half	1 tbsp.	20
whipping	1 tbsp.	55
light, coffee, or table	1 tbsp.	30
sour, dairy	1 tbsp.	29
Cucumber		
raw, whole	1 (7½″x2″)	30
raw, sliced	6 slices (⅛″ thick)	5
Custard, baked, with whole milk	1 cup	285

762

Dates, dry		
diced	1 cup	490
whole	5	100
Doughnuts, cake type	1	125
Duck, roast	3 slices (each 3½″x2½″x¼″)	165

Egg, whole	1	80
white	1	15
yolk	1	60
Eggplant, fried	1 slice (4″ diameter)	139

Endive		
Belgian	1 stalk	10
curly or chicory, broken	1 cup	5
escarole	2 leaves	5

Farina, cooked	1 cup	100
Figs		
fresh	3 small	90
canned, in syrup	½ cup	150
canned, diet-pack	½ cup	100
dried	2 medium	100
Flounder, fillet		
fresh, poached	1 piece (4″x2″x1″)	170
frozen, poached	4 oz.	76
Flour		
all-purpose, enriched, sifted	1 cup	400
cake or pastry, sifted	1 cup	365
self-rising, enriched	1 cup	385
whole-wheat	1 cup	400
Frankfurter (10 per lb.)	1	120
French dressing		
low-calorie	1 tbsp.	22
regular	1 tbsp.	50
Fruitcake, dark	1 piece (2″x2″x½″)	115
Fruit cocktail		
canned, in syrup	1 cup	195
canned, diet-pack	1 cup	88

Gelatin, unflavored	1 tbsp. (1 envelope)	35
Gelatin dessert, flavored, ready-to-eat		
regular	½ cup	81
low-calorie	½ cup	10
Gin	2 oz.	105
Ginger ale	1 bottle (7 oz.)	70
Gingerbread	1 piece (2″x2″x2″)	175
Grapefruit		
fresh	½ medium	55
sections, white	1 cup	75
canned		
sections, white	1 cup	175
diet-pack	1 cup	70
Grapefruit juice		
fresh	1 cup	95
canned, sweetened	1 cup	130
canned, unsweetened	1 cup	100
frozen concentrate, sweetened	6-oz. can	350
reconstituted	1 cup	115
frozen concentrate, unsweetened	6-oz. can	300
reconstituted	1 cup	100
Grapes, fresh		
Concord, Delaware, Niagara, Catawaba, Scuppernong	1 cup	65
Malaga, Muscat, Thompson seedless, Emperor, Flame Tokay	1 cup	95
Grape juice, bottled or canned	1 cup	165

Haddock		
fresh, broiled	1 piece (4″x3″x½″)	100

frozen, broiled	4 oz.	88
frozen, fish sticks, breaded	5	280
Halibut		
fresh, broiled	1 piece (4″x3″x¾″)	217
frozen, broiled	4 oz.	144
Ham		
baked	1 slice (5½″x3½″x ¼″)	253
boiled, sliced	2 oz.	135
Herring		
pickled	2 oz.	127
Hominy grits, cooked	1 cup	120
Honey, strained	1 tbsp.	65
Honeydew melon	⅛ medium	73
cubes	1 cup	58

I

Ice cream, commercial		
chocolate	⅔ cup	200
vanilla	⅔ cup	193
Ice cream, brick	1 slice or ⅛ quart	145
Ice milk		
chocolate	⅔ cup	144
vanilla	⅔ cup	136

J and K

Jams, jellies, preserves	1 tbsp.	55
Kale, cooked	1 cup	30
Kidney, cooked		
beef	3 oz.	118
lamb	3 oz.	111
pork	3 oz.	130

L

Lamb		
chop		
loin	6 oz. raw	223
rib	5 oz. raw	240
shoulder	5 oz. raw	252
roast, leg	1 slice (4″x4″x¼″)	165
shank	10 oz. raw	275
Lard	1 tbsp.	125
Leeks, chopped, cooked	½ cup	25
Lettuce, all varieties		
head	1 pound	47
shredded	1 cup	15
Lemon	1 medium	20
Lemonade concentrate		
frozen, sweetened	6-oz. can	430
reconstituted	1 cup	110
Lemon juice		
fresh	1 tbsp.	5
	1 cup	60
Limeade concentrate		
frozen, sweetened	6-oz. can	410
reconstituted	1 cup	105
Lime juice		
fresh	1 tbsp.	4
	1 cup	65
Liqueurs	1 oz.	165
Liver, cooked		
beef	3 oz.	117
calf's	3 oz.	136
lamb	3 oz.	171
pork	3 oz.	115
Liverwurst	1 slice (4″ diameter x¼″ thick)	100

Lobster		
fresh, boiled	¾ lb. in shell	108
canned, meat	½ cup	80
	5-oz. can	134
frozen, tails, boiled	3 small	81

M

Macaroni, cooked	1 cup	155
Macaroni and cheese, baked	1 cup	470
Mandarin orange segments,		
canned, in syrup	⅓ cup	55
canned, diet-pack	⅓ cup	24
Mango	1 medium	133
Manhattan	1 cocktail glass (2½ oz.)	165
Margarine	1 tbsp.	100
Martini	1 cocktail glass (2½ oz.)	145
Mayonnaise	1 tbsp.	100
low calorie	1 tbsp.	24
Melba toast	1 slice (3½″x1½″)	17
Milk		
buttermilk, from skim milk	1 cup	90
skim	1 cup	90
whole	1 cup	160
condensed, sweetened	1 cup	980
dry, instant nonfat	1 cup	250
evaporated	1 cup	345
Mixed vegetables, frozen, cooked	½ cup	55
Molasses	1 tbsp.	50
Muffins, plain	1 (2¾″)	140
Mushrooms		
fresh	6 large	14
canned(mushrooms and liquid)	1 cup	40
frozen, raw	14 caps	10
Mustard, prepared	1 tsp.	4

N

Nectarines	1 medium	50
Noodles, egg, cooked	1 cup	200

O

Oat cereal, ready-to-eat	1 cup	100
Oatmeal, regular or quick-cooking	1 cup	130
Okra		
fresh, cooked	8 pods	25
frozen, sliced, cooked	½ cup	26
Olives		
green, unpitted	4 medium	15
ripe, unpitted	2 large	15
Olive oil	1 tbsp.	125
Onion		
green	6 small	20
raw, whole	1 medium	40
raw, chopped	1 cup	60
Onion soup mix, dry	1 envelope or can	150
Orange		
fresh	1 medium	70
sections	½ cup	50
Orange juice		
fresh	1 cup	110
canned, unsweetened	1 cup	120

763

frozen concentrate, sweetened	6-oz. can	330
reconstituted	1 cup	110
Oysters, raw	13-19 medium	160
Oyster stew	3 to 4 oysters, ¼ cup oyster liquor, and ½ cup whole milk	200

P

Pancakes		
buckwheat, (pancake mix, with egg and milk)	1 cake (4″ diameter)	55
plain, home recipe	1 cake (4″ diameter)	60
Papaya, fresh, cubed	1 cup	70
Parsley, fresh, chopped	1 tbsp.	1
Parsnips, cooked, diced	1 cup	100
Peaches		
fresh, whole	1 medium	35
fresh, sliced, unsweetened	1 cup	65
canned, in syrup	2 halves and 2 tbsp. syrup	90
canned, diet-pack	2 halves and 2 tbsp. syrup	54
dried, uncooked	1 cup	420
cooked, unsweetened	1 cup (10 to 12 halves)	220
frozen, sweetened	⅓ cup	99
Peach nectar, canned	1 cup	120
Peanuts, roasted, salted	20 medium	100
chopped	1 tbsp.	55
dry-roasted	¼ cup	170
Peanut butter	1 tbsp.	95
Pears		
fresh, whole	1 medium	100
canned, in syrup	2 halves and 2 tbsp. syrup	90
canned, diet-pack	2 halves and 2 tbsp. syrup	44
Pear nectar, canned	1 cup	130
Peas, blackeye, frozen, cooked	½ cup	95
Peas, green		
fresh, cooked	1 cup	115
canned	1 cup	146
frozen, cooked	½ cup	60
Peas and carrots, frozen, cooked	½ cup	45
Pecans, halves	12	100
	½ cup	376
Peppers, sweet		
green, raw	1 medium	15
green, raw, diced	½ cup	16
red, raw	1 medium	20
Persimmons	1 medium	75
Pickles		
dill	1 (5″)	15
sweet	1 (3″)	30
Pies		
apple	⅛ of a 9″ pie	290
blueberry	⅛ of a 9″ pie	255
cherry	⅛ of a 9″ pie	299
custard	⅛ of a 9″ pie	233
lemon meringue	⅛ of a 9″ pie	264
mince	⅛ of a 9″ pie	298
pecan	⅛ of a 9″ pie	479
pumpkin	⅛ of a 9″ pie	230
Pimientos, canned	1 medium	10

764

Pine nuts (pignolias)	½ cup	671
Pineapple		
fresh, diced	1 cup	75
canned, crushed, in syrup	1 cup	195
canned, sliced, in syrup	2 small slices or 1 large and 2 tbsp. syrup	90
canned, tidbits, diet-pack	1 cup	151
frozen, cubes	1 cup	200
Pineapple juice		
canned	1 cup	135
frozen, reconstituted	1 cup	125
Plums		
fresh, whole	1 medium	25
canned, in syrup	3 plums and 2 tbsp. syrup	100
canned, diet-pack	3 plums and 2 tbsp. syrup	43
Pork		
chop		
rib	6 oz. raw	250
loin	6 oz. raw	283
roast, loin	1 chop (1″ thick)	330
luncheon meat	2 oz.	165
Popcorn, popped, with oil and salt	1 cup	65
Potatoes		
baked, without skin	1 medium	90
boiled, peeled after boiling	1 medium	105
boiled, pared before boiling	1 medium	80
French fried	10 pieces (each 2″x½″x½″)	155
French fried, frozen, heated only	10 pieces	125
mashed, with milk only	½ cup	70
Potato chips	10 (2″ diam.)	115
Prunes	4 medium	70
cooked, unsweetened	17-18 medium and ⅓ cup juice	295
canned, diet-pack	½ cup or 4 prunes and 3 tbsp. juice	128
Prune juice, canned or bottled	1 cup	200
Pumpkin, canned	1 cup	75

R

Radishes	4 small	5
Raisins	1 cup	460
Raspberries, red	1 cup	70
fresh	½ cup	100
canned, in syrup	½ cup	75
canned, diet-pack	½ cup	115
frozen, sweetened		
Rhubarb, cooked with sugar	1 cup	385
Rice, cooked		
brown	⅔ cup	100
precooked, cooked	⅔ cup	140
white	1 cup	185
wild	½ cup	73
Rice cereal, ready to eat	1 cup	115
Rice, puffed	1 cup	55
Rolls		
frankfurter	1	120
French	1 (4″x2″x2″)	118
hamburger	1 (3½″ diameter)	123
Parker house	1 (3″x2″x1½″)	114
Rum	2 ounces	105

Rutabagas, cubed, cooked	½ cup	25
Rye wafers	3 rectangular	63

S

Salad dressings		
blue cheese		
low-calorie	1 tbsp.	15
regular	1 tbsp.	80
French		
low-calorie	1 tbsp.	23
regular	1 tbsp.	60
mayonnaise		
low-calorie	1 tbsp.	24
regular	1 tbsp.	100
regular salad dressing	1 tbsp.	65
Thousand Island		
low-calorie	1 tbsp.	33
regular	1 tbsp.	75
Salad oil	1 tbsp.	125
Salami	3 slices (each 3¼"x⅛")	130
Salmon		
fresh, steak, broiled	1 piece (6"x3"x1")	430
canned	½ cup	120
Sardines, canned, in oil	4	100
Sauerkraut, canned	1 cup	32
Scallops, sea		
fresh, steamed	6 medium	105
frozen, steamed	1 cup	210
Sesame seeds	1 tbsp.	10
Sherbet, orange, milk	1 cup	260
Shortening, vegetable	1 tbsp.	110
Shredded wheat biscuit	1 (regular size)	94
Shrimps		
fresh, poached	7 medium	100
canned	5-oz. can	167
frozen, poached	9 medium	100
cocktail, tiny, canned	15	33
Sole, fillet		
fresh, poached	1 piece (4"x3½"x½")	177
frozen, poached	4 oz.	88
Soups, canned condensed, prepared with water, following label directions		
asparagus, cream of	1 cup	51
bean with pork	1 cup	130
beef broth	1 cup	22
beef noodle	1 cup	55
black bean	1 cup	80
celery, cream of	1 cup	75
cheese	1 cup	142
chicken, cream of	1 cup	85
chicken gumbo	1 cup	48
chicken noodle	1 cup	54
chicken vegetable	1 cup	60
chicken with rice	1 cup	44
chili beef	1 cup	133
clam chowder	1 cup	60
consomme	1 cup	25
green pea, cream of	1 cup	110
madrilene	1 cup	27
minestrone	1 cup	85
mushroom, cream of	1 cup	113
onion	1 cup	52
pepper pot	1 cup	83
potato, cream of	1 cup	59
Scotch broth	1 cup	74
split pea	1 cup	130
tomato	1 cup	73
tomato rice	1 cup	82
turkey noodle	1 cup	65
turkey vegetable	1 cup	58
vegetable	1 cup	63
vegetable beef	1 cup	61
Soups, condensed, frozen, prepared with water, following label directions		
clam chowder	1 cup	108
green pea with ham	1 cup	109
oyster stew	1 cup	102
potato, cream of	1 cup	90
shrimp, cream of	1 cup	132
Soups, packaged mix prepared with water, following label directions		
beef	1 cup	87
beef noodle	1 cup	70
chicken noodle	1 cup	60
chicken rice	1 cup	55
green pea	1 cup	128
mushroom, cream of	1 cup	46
onion	1 cup	40
potato, cream of	1 cup	90
tomato vegetable	1 cup	69
vegetable	1 cup	69
Soybean oil	1 tbsp.	125
Spaghetti, cooked	1 cup	155
Spinach		
fresh, cooked	1 cup	40
canned	1 cup	45
frozen, chopped or leaf	½ cup	24
Squash, yellow, zucchini, crookneck, patty pan,		
sliced, cooked	1 cup	30
frozen, cooked	½ cup	20
Squash, hubbard, acorn, banana,		
baked, mashed	1 cup	130
frozen, cooked	½ cup	50
Strawberries		
fresh	1 cup	55
frozen		
whole, sweetened	⅔ cup	131
whole, unsweetened	1 cup	55
sliced, sweetened	½ cup	140
Succotash, frozen, cooked	½ cup	87
Sugars		
brown, firmly packed	1 cup	820
	1 tbsp.	57
granulated	1 cup	770
	1 tbsp.	45
lump	1 (1⅛"x¾"x⅜")	25
10X (confectioners' powdered)	1 cup	495
	1 tbsp.	30
Sweet potatoes		
baked, without skin	1 medium	155
boiled, peeled after boiling	1 medium	170
canned, without syrup	1 cup	235
Swordfish		
fresh broiled, with little butter or margarine	1 slice (3"x3"x½")	150
frozen, broiled, with little butter or margarine	1 slice (3"x3"x½")	150
Syrup		
corn, light or dark	1 tbsp.	60
maple	1 tbsp.	61
maple-blended	1 tbsp.	54
pancake	1 tbsp.	55

T

Tangerine	1 large	40
Tangerine juice, canned, unsweetened	1 cup	105
Tapioca, quick-cooking, uncooked	1 tbsp.	35
Tomatoes		
fresh	1 medium	35
canned	1 cup	50
Tomato juice, canned	1 cup	45
Tuna		
canned, in oil, drained	½ cup	170
canned, in water	½ cup	109
Turnips, white cooked, diced	1 cup	35
Turkey, roast	1 slice breast (4″x2½″x¼″)	134
Turkey TV dinner	1 dinner	375

V

Veal		
chop		
loin	8 oz. raw	251
rib	6 oz. raw	240
roast, leg	1 slice (5″x4″x¼″)	159
scallopini, sauteed	3 pieces (each 3½″x2″x⅛″)	172
Vinegar	1 tbsp.	2

W

Walnuts, English		
chopped	1 tbsp.	50
halves	1 cup	650
Watermelon, fresh	1 wedge (4″x4″x8″)	115
cubed	1 cup	40
Wheat cereal, cooked	1 cup	175
flakes, ready-to-eat	1 cup	100
puffed	1⅓ cups	105
presweetened	¾ cup	105
shredded	1 biscuit (regular size)	94
Wheat germ	1 tbsp.	27
Whiskey	2 ounces	105
Wine		
dry	3 oz.	85
sweet	3 oz.	160

Y and Z

Yams, pared, cubed, cooked	½ cup	90
Yogurt		
skim milk	1 cup	120
whole milk	1 cup	176
Zwieback	1 slice	31

INDEX TO RECIPES IN THIS VOLUME

767

768